GW00367894

The West Country

Published by VisitBritain

Published by VisitBritain Publishing
Thames Tower, Blacks Road, London W6 9EL

First published 2007

ISBN 978 0 7095 8401 8
Product code: SBTR03

A CIP catalogue record for this book is available from the British Library.

Produced for VisitBritain Publishing by Departure Lounge Limited
Contributing authors: Etain O'Carroll, Charmian Rex, Nick Rider,
Andrew Stone, Nick Traynor
Cartography: Cosmographics (pages 8–9); Draughtsman Maps;
Reprographics by Blaze Creative
Printed and bound in the UK by Stones The Printers

Jacket: Main image: Oare, Exmoor, Somerset
Top inset image: Levant, Cornwall
Bottom inset image: Durdle Door, Dorset
Title page: Perranporth, Cornwall **Pages 4–5:** Tarr Steps, Exmoor National Park

Contents

The West Country

Our tours of the West Country sweep you across rolling hills and through brooding moorland to stunning coastal scenery and pretty fishing villages in search of legend and folklore – and delicious cream teas. Discover bustling resorts and quiet, sandy coves, rugged cliffs and wide sandy beaches and perhaps pick up a fossil or two along the Jurassic Coast. Go in search of King Arthur at Tintagel, recall the plots of his novels as your drive through Thomas Hardy's 'Wessex' and spend a day following in Jane Austen's footsteps around the wonders of Georgian Bath.

Specialist travel writers have crafted the 10 guided driving tours in this book to cover circular routes of two to four days, which include famous and lesser-known sights alike. The itineraries can be joined at any point along the way or easily linked to shape a longer journey and, where appropriate, each itinerary also suggests ways to extend your trip with scenic walks, tours on heritage railways and boat trips.

The Tours

This guide contains a selection of special driving itineraries plotted on detailed maps. These circular routes can be joined at any point to explore as many places each day as you wish. The short descriptions highlight places of interest within each tour whilst tinted boxes feature information on related people, events and stories. A final box also suggests places off the route that are worth a detour. Remember, it is also a good idea to makes use of available park-and-ride schemes for popular places and attractions.

Introduction
Each tour has a short introduction that gives a flavour of the area covered by the tour route.

Tour map
Each route is plotted on the tour map in blue. Blue numbered bullets correspond to the number of each entry and the name is labelled in blue. Places mentioned in the 'with more time' box are also labelled in blue – and where located off the map, are arrowed off.

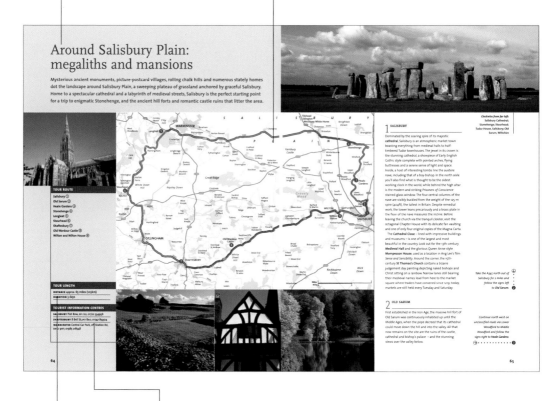

Approximate length of tour in distance and duration.

Selected Tourist Information Centres in the area.

Overleaf you will find a simple map of the region showing the location of all the tours. Each has been cross-referenced to page so you can turn straight to your chosen itinerary. In each case, the start of the tour is clearly marked by a light grey circle.

Feature boxes
The story behind selected places; literary and historical links; local legends and heroes; or suggested walks and cycle rides.

Picture captions
A single caption describes the images on each spread; boxed images are explained in the relevant box.

WOODFORD VALLEY TRAIL
North of Salisbury lies the Woodford Valley, renowned for its charming, riverside thatched cottages. Though it makes a pleasant drive, it is best appreciated on foot, and there is an easy, circular waymarked route that wanders through the valley from Upper Woodford, taking about three hours to complete. Head north from the Bridge Inn in Upper Woodford through a small wood and along the river to the picturesque villages of Great Durnford and Wilsford. From here the trail leads to Normanton Down where you can explore ancient burial mounds and take in fabulous views over Stonehenge. The route then circles back to Upper Woodford. A second, shorter trail starts in Lower Woodford and explores the lower river valley passing thatched homes, quaint estate cottages and a manor house en route.

Clockwise from far left:
Gold Hill, Shaftesbury;
Cube Room, Wilton House;
Palladian bridge,
Wilton House

Take the A350 south and turn left onto the A30. Head east for 6 miles until the signposted turning on the left to Old Wardour Castle.

7 SHAFTESBURY
Lording it over the surrounding plains, the town of Shaftesbury is perched on an outcrop of sandstone and offers brilliant views over Blackmore Vale. At the height of its fortunes, the town boasted a castle, 12 churches and four market crosses. Its most famous attraction today is charming Gold Hill, a steep, curving cobbled street of thatched cottages used as a film location in *Far from the Madding Crowd* and in the classic Hovis bread advert. To see inside one of the quaint cottages pop into the Shaftesbury Town Museum, where you can also gain insight on the history of the town and its abbey. Once the richest nunnery in England, Shaftesbury Abbey was founded by Alfred the Great in AD888 and razed by Henry VIII 650 years later. Today only the foundations remain.

Continue travelling north east on the A30 to Wilton. Wilton House is signposted to the right off the round-about on Minster Street.

8 OLD WARDOUR CASTLE
One of the most romantic ruins in England, Old Wardour Castle has a stunning lakeside setting and a bloody, tormented past. Made famous by Kevin Costner's *Robin Hood: Prince of Thieves*, the unique six-sided castle was originally built by Lord Lovel in the 14th century and took its inspiration from French chateaux. By the early 17th century, it was the royalist Arundell family who ruled the roost, and in 1643 some 1,300 advancing Parliamentarians besieged the castle with only Lady Blanche Arundell and 25 men to defend it. They managed to hold out for almost one month before the castle was captured; the lady of the house was imprisoned and later executed. Six months on, a countersiege began, which ended only when gunpowder mines under the castle exploded and destroyed it beyond repair. The ruined castle soon became a backdrop for a new house, but to this day Lady Arundell's ghost is said to wander the castle ruins at twilight.

9 WILTON AND WILTON HOUSE
Renowned for its carpet industry, the quaint market town of Wilton was once the ancient capital of Wessex and today makes a pleasant stopping-off point for its Georgian houses, riverside walk and numerous antique shops. Its real gem, however, is the exquisite Wilton House, home to the earls of Pembroke since 1542. The house was rebuilt by Indigo Jones after a major fire in 1643 and its sumptuous interiors feature elaborate plasterwork, ornate ceilings and a host of paintings by Van Dyck, Rembrandt, Poussin and Tintoretto. The beautiful gardens have attracted numerous film-makers: scenes from *The Madness of King George* and *Mrs Brown* were shot here, and the stunning Double Cube Room appears as the ballroom in *Sense and Sensibility*.

Leave Wilton heading east on the A36 to return to Salisbury.

WITH MORE TIME
If time permits, extend your route north via the sleepy village of Tilshead to look at its distinctive flint and stone buildings. Continue to Edington, where the priory – all that is left of a 14th-century Augustinian monastery – beautifully exemplifies the architectural transition from Decorated to Perpendicular style, with an unusual two-storey porch, medieval marble floors, Victorian mosaics and fine plaster ceilings. To the west in Bratton, you can stretch your legs on a steep climb to the Westbury White Horse (left; see p775), which dates from the 18th century.

68

69

Directions
A suggested route between consecutive entries is provided. You might also like to use a full road atlas to check minor roads.

Entry description
The numbered entries explore some of the area's key attractions.

With more time box
This offers suggestions for places and attractions that are off the route but worth exploring if you have more time.

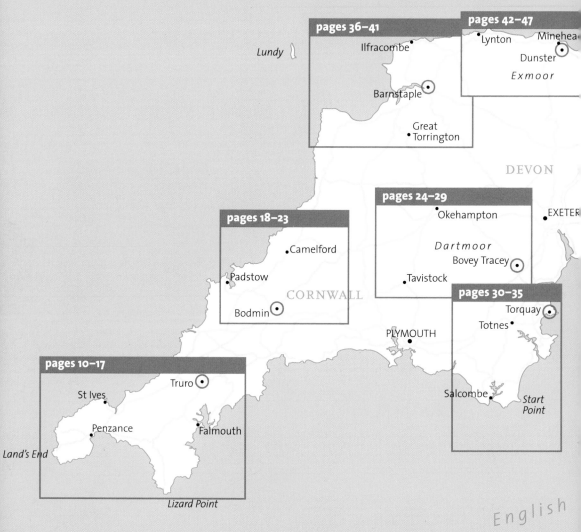

Bristol Channel

Lundy

pages 36–41

Ilfracombe

pages 42–47

Lynton

Minehead

Dunster

Exmoor

Barnstaple

Great
Torrington

DEVON

pages 24–29

Okehampton

EXETER

Dartmoor

Bovey Tracey

pages 18–23

Camelford

Tavistock

pages 30–35

Padstow

Torquay

CORNWALL

Totnes

Bodmin

PLYMOUTH

pages 10–17

Truro

St Ives

Salcombe

*Start
Point*

Penzance

Falmouth

Land's End

Lizard Point

English

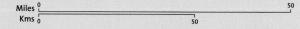

Miles 0   50
Kms 0   50

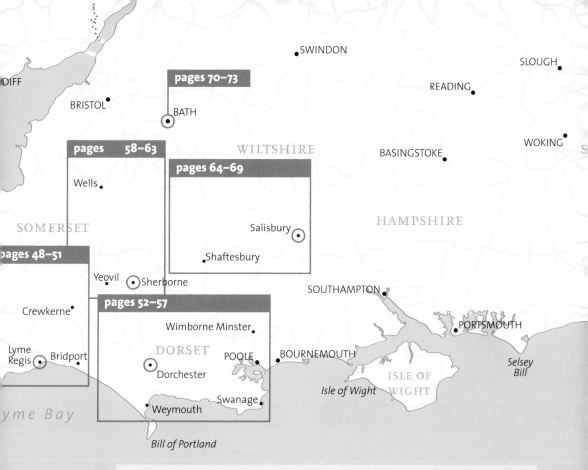

SWINDON

SLOUGH

DIFF

READING

pages 70–73

BRISTOL

WOKING

BATH

WILTSHIRE

BASINGSTOKE

pages 58–63

pages 64–69

Wells

HAMPSHIRE

SOMERSET

Salisbury

pages 48–51

Shaftesbury

Yeovil ⊙ Sherborne

SOUTHAMPTON

pages 52–57

PORTSMOUTH

Crewkerne

Wimborne Minster

Lyme
Regis

Bridport

DORSET

POOLE

BOURNEMOUTH

Selsey
Bill

Dorchester

ISLE OF

Swanage

Isle of Wight

WIGHT

yme Bay

Weymouth

Bill of Portland

THE TOURS

The West Country

nannel

Along the rugged Cornish coast

The spectacular Atlantic Ocean crashes relentlessly onto the dramatic coastline of north Cornwall, a land steeped in folklore and alive with tales of smugglers and giants. Here gaunt tin mine engine houses – testimony to a once flourishing mining industry – tower above golden sandy beaches that are a magnet for thrill-seeking surfers. Along the gentler south coast are shady creeks, unspoilt bays and timeless fishing villages where colour-washed cottages tumble to the harbours below. The intense quality of the light in this part of the country has made the area a magnet for painters and artists since the early 19th century.

TOUR ROUTE

Truro ①
Portloe and Veryan ②
St Mawes ③
Falmouth and Trelissick Garden ④
Trebah and Glendurgan gardens ⑤
Gweek and Helford ⑥
Coverack ⑦
Cadgwith ⑧
Lizard ⑨
Mullion Cove, Poldhu and Gunwalloe ⑩
Marazion and St Michael's Mount ⑪
Penzance and Newlyn ⑫
Mousehole ⑬
Porthcurno ⑭
Land's End and Sennen Cove ⑮
St Just ⑯
Zennor ⑰
St Ives ⑱

TOUR LENGTH

DISTANCE approx. 170 miles (274km)

DURATION 4 days

TOURIST INFORMATION CENTRES

PENZANCE Station Rd, TR18 2NF;
01736 362207

ST IVES The Guildhall, Street-an-Pol,
TR26 2DS; 01736 796297

TRURO Municipal Building, Boscawen St,
TR1 2NE; 01872 27455

1 TRURO

The wealth of grand Georgian mansions in Truro are testimony to this small city's former role as a significant port and mining centre. Particularly fine architectural examples can be found on Lemon Street and Walsingham Place. Dominating the town centre is **Truro Cathedral**, built in the Gothic revival style on the site of the church of St Mary the Virgin and completed in 1910. Part of the original church is incorporated in the new building, where the spacious vaulted interior features some impressive stained glass, among the finest in the country. Look out for the heavily carved reredos behind the altar and splendid font of polished porphyry. Other treasures include a copy of a letter from Charles I thanking the Cornish for their loyalty during the Civil War. From the cathedral, amble around the cobbled streets and picturesque alleyways or 'opes' – with amusing names like Squeezeguts Alley – that have survived from Truro's heyday as a port. Then pay a visit to the excellent **Royal Cornwall Museum**, which explores Cornwall's history and features works from the Newlyn School of artists *(see p14)*. Afterwards you can stroll along the Riverside Walk and watch the passenger boats cruising down the river, or make the most of Truro's excellent shopping centre, two covered markets and the range of specialist shops on Lemon Quay.

*Head east on the A39/A390.
At Tresillian turn right onto
unclassified roads through
Ruan Lanihorne, crossing
over the A3078 to **Portloe**
and then **Veryan**.*

2 PORTLOE AND VERYAN

Dramatically set in a break in the cliffs, with white-washed cottages clustering round a tiny harbour, **Portloe** is one of Cornwall's most unspoilt and photo-genic fishing hamlets. The village hotel, set right at the water's edge, is an ideal spot for a contemplative drink.

Just a short distance inland from Portloe lies the village of **Veryan**, famous for its five circular thatched cottages topped by crosses. The unusual 19th-century houses were designed to ward off the devil, who, it was thought, would be unable to hide if there were no corners.

*Continue west on
unclassified roads to the
A3078 and turn left to
St Mawes.*

Catch the car ferry across
the estuary from St Mawes
to *Falmouth*. Return by
ferry to your car and exit St
Mawes on the A3078. Turn
left onto the B3289 and
cross the River Fal on the
King Harry Ferry to
④ *Trelissick Garden*.

Continue west on the
B3289, turning left onto
unclassified roads through
Penpol to the A39 and then
left again. On reaching
Mabe Burnthouse, take
unclassified roads south
to *Trebah* and
⑤ *Glendurgan gardens*.

Drive west on unclassified
roads via Porth Navas to
Gweek. Continue round
the head of the River
Helford to Mawgan then
east to *Helford*.

→ • • • • • • • • ⑥

3 ST MAWES

Dazzling white yachts bob in the harbour of this
fashionable sailing mecca, which boasts fine estuary
views and a network of inland waterways. The pretty
waterfront leads west to the well-preserved clover-leaf
St Mawes Castle, built by Henry VIII (together with its
twin, Pendennis, across the water) to guard the
entrance into Carrick Roads Estuary. From here there is
a lovely two-mile walk north along the water's edge to
St Just in Roseland. The ancient church here, set in lush,
tropical gardens, was described by poet John Betjeman
as 'the most beautiful (churchyard) on earth'.

4 FALMOUTH AND TRELISSICK GARDEN

Regular ferries run across the estuary from St Mawes
to the old seafaring town of **Falmouth**. This is a place
of great vistas, and it's well worth climbing the 110
steps known as Jacob's Ladder for a bird's eye view of
the harbour, as well as exploring **Pendennis Castle**, set
on a headland with sweeping panoramas.

The town's excellent **National Maritime Museum
Cornwall**, housed in swanky new waterfront premises,
boasts a huge collection of boats of all sizes, as well as
lots of interactive exhibits, audio-visual displays and a
29-m tall tower (95ft) affording fantastic views over the
harbour and estuary. Return to St Mawes and continue
by road to the peaceful **Trelissick Garden**, 210ha (525
acres) of stunning parkland and woods, famed for its
hydrangeas and camellias.

5 TREBAH AND GLENDURGAN GARDENS

The peaceful wooded River Helford and its numerous
secretive creeks are blessed with a mild climate that
allows sub-tropical gardens to flourish. It provides the
setting for the wild and enchanting **Trebah Garden**,
nestled in a steep ravine where a stream cascades
through rhododendrons, tree ferns and huge, menacing
gunnera to the River Helford below. Just as magical is
Glendurgan Garden, with its restored laurel maze and
winding paths leading down through exotic plant
species to the miniscule fishing village of Durgan,
where boats cluster on the tiny beach.

6 GWEEK AND HELFORD

At the head of the River Helford is the small port of **Gweek** with its delightful clutter of boatyards and the **National Seal Sanctuary**, where injured seals and sea lions are nursed to health before being released back into the wild. Further east is **Helford** with its pretty whitewashed cottages and a thatched pub. From here, follow the signposted footpath to Frenchman's Creek: this mysterious winding inlet was the inspiration for – and title of – Daphne du Maurier's romantic tale of piracy and smuggling.

7 COVERACK

The tiny harbour at pretty Coverack, once the haunt of smugglers and pirates, provides one of the few safe havens on this unforgiving shore. The photographs in the bar of the Paris Hotel (named after an American liner wrecked offshore) show just how devastating a storm off this stretch of coast can be.

8 CADGWITH

Drivers need their wits about them when navigating the steep lanes down into this picturesque little fishing village, crammed haphazardly with old thatched cottages. Cadgwith is the perfect spot to indulge in an afternoon tea before taking a short walk along the coast to the Devil's Frying Pan, a collapsed blowhole – its name takes on real meaning when the sea is rough.

Clockwise from far left:
St Mawes Castle; Lizard
Peninsula; Trebah Garden

A CHANGE OF PACE

For a more leisurely pace, abandon the car and take to the **South West Coast Path**, which provides some of the most exhilarating and scenic coastal walking in Britain, particularly around Lizard Point *(below)* and Land's End (check www.southwestcoastpath.com for recommended walks). Alternatively, swap four wheels for two on the flat plateau of the **Lizard Peninsula**, which is ideal for lazy cycling, especially in spring when wild daffodils, bluebells and primroses carpet the roadside banks.

9 LIZARD

Lizard does a brisk trade in souvenirs made from local serpentine, which, when cut and polished, was much admired by Queen Victoria. Stroll down to the dramatic cliffs of **Lizard Point**, the most southerly point in mainland Britain, and take in the awe-inspiring views from the top of the lighthouse, whose powerful beam is visible 26 miles away. On a sunny day, it's worth making the short journey to nearby **Kynance Cove**, a renowned beauty spot with golden sands and glistening rock pools.

*Travel south on unclassified roads via St Anthony and St Keverne to the B3294 and turn left to **Coverack**.* **7**

*Take the unclassified road to the B3293 and turn left. After about 2 miles turn left onto the unclassified road south to **Cadgwith**.* **8**

*Leave Cadgwith on unclassified roads to join the A3083 and turn left to **Lizard**.* **9**

*Travel north on the A3083, and turn left on the B3296 via Mullion to **Mullion Cove**. Return to Mullion and turn left to **Poldhu**. From here follow unclassified roads north and turn left on the A3083. Shortly after turn left on the unclassified road to **Gunwalloe**.*

 **10**

10 MULLION COVE, POLDHU AND GUNWALLOE

Drive north east to the A3083 and turn left. At Helston take the A394 west and after about 8 miles **11** *turn left to **Marazion**.*

To the west of the bustling inland village of Mullion are a succession of little coves, strung out like pearls along the coast. The pretty weather-worn harbour of **Mullion Cove** is a National Trust gem; to its north the sandy bay of **Poldhu** has a simple cliff-top monument marking the spot where Marconi transmitted the first wireless message across the Atlantic in 1901; and further north still, tiny **Gunwalloe** is blessed with a 15th-century church set among the sand dunes.

11 MARAZION AND ST MICHAEL'S MOUNT

*Drive west on the unclassified road to join the A30, then turn left into **Penzance**. From here, travel along the Esplanade to **Newlyn**.*

First granted a charter in 1257, Marazion is one of Cornwall's oldest chartered towns and was the most important settlement around Mount's Bay until the late Middle Ages. The busy main street is lined with shops and galleries, while the golden sandy beach is a magnet for windsurfers. Behind the beach, the RSPB's **Marazion Marsh Nature Reserve** is a popular spot with birdwatchers.

At low tide a cobbled causeway leads from Marazion to the magical rocky islet of **St Michael's Mount**, crowned dramatically by its medieval castle and priory built on the site of a Benedictine monastery. At high tide the islet is accessible only by ferry. From the landing stage, a steep path leads up to the impressive castle. Highlights of a visit include the Chevy Chase Room, formerly the monks' refectory, and the Garrison Room from where the Spanish Armada was famously sighted in 1588.

12 PENZANCE AND NEWLYN

Penzance gained notoriety in 1595 when Spanish galleons appeared in the bay, and the town was sacked and burned. Today, most of the town's interesting buildings lie along winding Chapel Street, which leads down from the granite Market House (built in 1836), to the quay. Among those of particular note are the flamboyant 19th-century **Egyptian House** (No. 6–7), built in 1835 as a museum, and **No. 25**, home to Maria Branwell – mother to the famous authors, Charlotte, Emily and Anne Brontë – until 1812. Other sights of interest include the statue of Penzance-born Sir Humphrey Davy – the inventor of the eponymous miners' safety lamp – which sits at the top of the main Market Jew Street, and **Penlee House Gallery and Museum**, which exhibits works from the highly regarded Newlyn School of painting.

Newlyn is a lively little port that lies along the promenade about one mile south west of town. It gained fame when Stanhope Forbes came here to paint in 1884. Attracted by the exceptional quality of the light in the area, Forbes was soon joined by other painters and the Newlyn School was born. The town is still popular with artists, many of whom show their works in the **Newlyn Art Gallery**.

*Take the unclassified coast road south from Newlyn to **Mousehole**.*
→ • • • • • • • • • • • **13**

Clockwise from far left:
beach, Porthcurno; Minack
Theatre, Porthcurno; Land's
End; harbour, Penzance

13 MOUSEHOLE

It is wise to park on the outskirts of Mousehole and enter the village on foot, as the roads are narrow and parking is limited. This all adds to the undeniable charm of this lovely little fishing village, which clusters around its almost circular harbour. Nearby, Keighwin House is the only house to survive the 1595 Spanish raid. Mousehole is also famous as the home of Dolly Pentreath, the last person to speak the ancient Cornish language, which died with her some 200 years ago. Her memorial lies in the churchyard at **Paul**, a half-mile walk away.

14 PORTHCURNO

En route to Porthcurno, stop off just outside Lamorna, to see the stone circle of the **Merry Maidens**, reputedly all that remains of 19 local lasses turned to stone for dancing on the Sabbath. The two large stones of The Pipers nearby are thought to be the musicians who suffered the same fate. A few miles further west is the gorgeous beach of **Porthcurno** with its crystal-clear waters. It was here that the first transatlantic underground cable was laid, linking Britain to the rest of the world, and the story is told at the **Porthcurno Telegraph Museum**. Steep steps lead from the beach up to the **Minack Theatre**, a stunning open-air amphitheatre carved into the cliff. An evening performance here – with the moon shining and the waves lapping below – is pure magic. Even if you can't see a performance, it's worth visiting for the sweeping views over Porthcurno Bay and the visitor's centre telling the remarkable story of its founder, Rowena Cade.

15 LAND'S END AND SENNEN COVE

Tantalising sea views stretch from **Land's End** past wind-beaten outcrops and the Longships Lighthouse to the Wolf Rock Lighthouse, the beam of which is visible nine miles out to sea. England's westernmost tip has always been a tourist magnet, and there are visitor attractions aplenty here if that's what you're after. Along the coast, lies the pretty village of **Sennen Cove** where you can have an evening drink at the old inn before taking a barefoot stroll along the sandy beach as the sun sinks over the sea.

A FISHY TALE

During the Christmas festive season, lights are hung all around the village of Mousehole and even out to sea. One is in the shape of a 'Stargazey Pie', a local speciality made with whole fish and cooked each year on the 23rd of December. The tradition commemorates the dreadful winter night some 200 years ago when local fisherman Tom Bawcock braved terrible storms to bring home fish to feed the starving villagers.

Head south out of Mousehole and west to the B3315 and turn left. Stop off in the layby for the Merry Maidens then continue for about 4 miles and turn left for **Porthcurno**. **14**

Return to the B3315 and turn left to **Land's End**. *From here, travel north east on the A30 for about 2 miles and turn left for* **Sennen Cove**. **15**

Rejoin the A30 and turn left. After about 1 mile, turn left on the B3306 and left again on the A3071 to **St Just**. **16**

Take the B3306
following the coast north
⑰ east to **Zennor**.

16 ST JUST

Stark silhouettes of the entrances to abandoned tin mines dot the rugged landscape around St Just. One of the most spectacularly sited is **Botallack**, with its disused engine houses perched precariously on the cliffs. At **Geevor Tin Mine**, the harsh realities of a miner's existence are brought to life by a visit to its 18th-century 'adits' or tunnels, often only 1.5m high (5ft). Up until its closure in 1990 this was Cornwall's largest mine, extending far out under the sea.

17 ZENNOR

Zennor's low grey houses huddle together on a stretch of wild and windswept coast scattered with archae-ological remains and steeped in tales of folklore. One such tale involves a stone behind the church where it is said the benevolent Giant of Zennor would sit. He one day patted a man on the head, inadvertently cracking his skull, and the giant then died of a broken heart. The **Wayside Folk Museum** houses a rich collection of relics from this isolated little hamlet and is well worth a visit. Zennor's claim to fame is its connections to D H Lawrence, who lived here with his German wife during World War I, while writing *Women in Love*. He was driven away on suspicion of signalling to German U-Boats.

Continue on the B3306
east to **St Ives**.

→ • • • • • • • • • • ⑱

Clockwise from far left:
beach, St Ives; Tate Modern,
St Ives; Barbara Hepworth
Museum, St Ives; Botallack
tin mine, St Just

THE ST IVES SCHOOL

Following J M W Turner's first visit in 1811, the coming of the railways brought a wave of artists to St Ives. Whistler and Sickert were followed by the likes of Sir Alfred Munnings, Barbara Hepworth, Christopher Wood and Ben Nicholson. They converted the town's old pilchard cellars and sail lofts into studios and established the St Ives School, which flourished in the 1950s. It was Nicholson and Wood who discovered Alfred Wallis, probably Britain's best-known naïve artist, whose primitive maritime scenes were often rendered on scraps of driftwood. Nicholson, together with Russian Naum Gabo, also greatly influenced the work of St Ives-born Peter Lanyon, whose abstract work is inspired by the local landscape.

More recent artists with links to the town include Patrick Heron and Sir Terry Frost as well as Bryan Pearce, currently one of Britain's foremost naïve painters. The **St Ives Society of Artists**, founded in 1927, displays some excellent examples of local work in the Old Mariner's Church in Norway Square. Just outside St Ives, Higher Stennack is home to **Leach Pottery** (re-opening spring 2007) where Bernard Leach's Japanese-inspired ceramics are displayed alongside works of his contemporaries, including his associate Shoji Hamada.

18 ST IVES

The sheer beauty of this lovely fishing town – with its sandy beaches and steep alleyways clustered around the harbour – together with the incredibly intense light here has captivated artists since the early 1800s. Works of 20th-century St Ives painters including Ben Nicholson, Alfred Wallis and Peter Lanyon are among the modern art on display at the exceptional **Tate St Ives**. Spectacularly set above Porthmeor Beach, the sparkling white, modern building is an architectural delight in its own right. It houses changing displays from the Tate's national collection, as well as pottery by Bernard Leach and sculptures by Barbara Hepworth.

Nearby on Barnoon Hill is the **Barbara Hepworth Museum and Sculpture Garden**, where an impressive collection of the sculptor's works and all manner of memorabilia are on display in the studio where she lived until her tragic death in 1975. Her sculptures are also artistically exhibited in the adjoining garden.

As if this wasn't enough, St Ives also offers a plethora of private galleries and studios as well as some superb sandy beaches and bracing headland walks.

Take the A3074 south and
turn left on the B3301 to
Portreath. Continue on
unclassified roads through
Porthtowan to St Agnes,
then turn right on
the B3277/A390 to
return to Truro.

⊖ • • • • • • • • • • • ❶

WITH MORE TIME

It is well worth the expense of taking the 20-minute helicopter flight from Penzance across to the **Isles of Scilly**, where the pace of life is slow and gentle. The largest island, St Mary's, is only three miles wide and two miles long with ten miles of beautiful coastline. The next largest, Tresco, boasts fabulous beaches and is home to the sub-tropical Abbey Garden *(left)* and Valhalla Collection with its relics from shipwrecks. You can also fly to the islands from Land's End airport or hop on a ferry from Penzance, which takes just over two and a half hours.

The wilds of Bodmin Moor

The smallest of the West Country moors, spanning just ten miles in diameter, Bodmin Moor is a bleak and desolate wilderness scattered with rocky outcrops, eroded by years of wind and rain, and peppered with the remains of ancient civilisations. Further north, the dramatic Cornish coastline is characterised by windswept headlands, sweeping sea views, quintessential fishing harbours, picturesque resorts and historic houses, which have remained unchanged for centuries. Steeped in folklore and intriguing legends of King Arthur, the area's strong connection to Britain's ancient past adds to its infinite appeal.

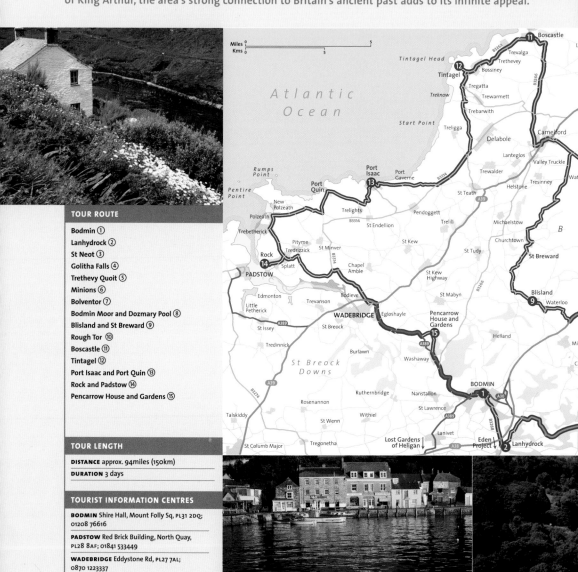

TOUR ROUTE

Bodmin ①
Lanhydrock ②
St Neot ③
Golitha Falls ④
Trethevy Quoit ⑤
Minions ⑥
Bolventor ⑦
Bodmin Moor and Dozmary Pool ⑧
Blisland and St Breward ⑨
Rough Tor ⑩
Boscastle ⑪
Tintagel ⑫
Port Isaac and Port Quin ⑬
Rock and Padstow ⑭
Pencarrow House and Gardens ⑮

TOUR LENGTH

DISTANCE approx. 94miles (150km)
DURATION 3 days

TOURIST INFORMATION CENTRES

BODMIN Shire Hall, Mount Folly Sq, PL31 2DQ;
01208 76616

PADSTOW Red Brick Building, North Quay,
PL28 8AF; 01841 533449

WADEBRIDGE Eddystone Rd, PL27 7AL;
0870 1223337

Clockwise from far left: cottage, Boscastle; Boscastle village; gatehouse, Lanhydrock; aerial view, Lanhydrock; harbour, Padstow

1 BODMIN

Situated on the old trade route between Ireland and the Continent, Bodmin was once an important resting point for Christian pilgrims, including St Petroc who founded a priory here in the 6th century. **St Petroc's Church** houses the ornate cask that once contained his relics and which has twice been stolen and returned.

Bodmin has many places to visit, including the **Military Museum**, **Bodmin Town Museum** and **Bodmin Jail**, where some of the nation's most precious possessions, including the Crown Jewels and the Domesday Book, were hidden during World War I. Grisly exhibits in the gloomy underground passages and prison cells recreate the unbearable conditions once endured here. All those who met their end here were buried in its grounds and an unmistakable air of despair still lingers. Among them was Matthew Weeks who was executed for murder in 1844. His trial can be relived at the **Courtroom Experience** housed in the nearby Shire Hall.

*Take the B3268 south from Bodmin and follow the signs to **Lanhydrock**. Alternatively, hop on the Bodmin and Wenford Steam Railway from Bodmin station to Bodmin Parkway, from where there is a pretty walk to Lanhydrock.* **2**

2 LANHYDROCK

This beautiful 17th-century country house was once part of St Petroc's Priory, and is set in 180ha (450 acres) of woods and parkland, which descend to the River Fowey. Magnificent formal gardens with clipped yews and terraces, stunning magnolias and circular herbaceous borders surround the house and the parish church. Fifty rooms of the house are open to the public – from the long gallery with its intricately carved plasterwork ceiling to the kitchen complex recalling life 'downstairs'.

*Follow the unclassified road north east to join the A38 and turn right heading east, then turn left after about 6 miles onto unclassified roads to **St Neot**.*

 3

- Follow the unclassified road east to
④ **Golitha Falls**.

- Continue on the unclassified road east towards Minions, turning right to Darite for
⑤ **Trethevy Quoit**.

- Return to Darite and proceed on unclassified roads west, then
⑥ north to **Minions**.

- Return past the turn off for Darite and turn right following the River Fowey
⑦ north to **Bolventor**.

- From the centre of Bolventor turn south onto the unclassified road to
⑧ **Dozmary Pool**.

Loop around Colliford Lake and head north to the A30, then turn left. After about 5 miles turn right following unclassified roads to **Blisland**. Then follow the unclassified roads north to **St Breward**.

→ • • • • • • • • • • ⑨

3 ST NEOT

This pretty little village is worth a detour for its 15th-century **church**, which contains the most complete set of medieval stained-glass windows in England. Perhaps the most interesting is the one depicting St Neot, the kindly dwarf after whom the village was named. Standing only 1.2m (4ft) tall, the saint was famed for the miracles he performed involving animals, several of which are illustrated in the stained glass. Look for the oak branch on the roof of the tower, which is renewed every Oak Apple Day to commemorate the village's support of the royalist cause during the Civil War. In the churchyard stand five historic carved crosses. The oldest dates from the 9th century and is one of the best preserved Cornish crosses. Also worth a look before leaving is **St Neot Pottery**.

4 GOLITHA FALLS

An ideal spot to stop and stretch your legs, this nature reserve is set around an area of ancient woodland, which clings to the sides of a steep gorge where the River Fowey tumbles down a series of cascades. The scenery here is beautiful at any time of the year, but the falls are at their best after a bout of heavy rain. There are plenty of waymarked walks to follow through the oak and ash woods.

5 TRETHEVY QUOIT

This imposing Bronze Age burial chamber is known locally as the Giant's House and dates from about 3500BC. The megalithic chamber is constructed from five huge granite slabs surmounted by a capstone. A small natural hole in the capstone may have been used for astronomical observations, while the rectangular hole chiselled out of the entrance stone is thought to have been used to entomb the bodies.

6 MINIONS

The quiet moorland village of Minions, the highest in Cornwall, was once a thriving mining centre for granite, copper and lead. Its history is explained in the **Minions Heritage Centre**, housed in a former engine house. A short walk west leads to the three stone circles of the **Hurlers**, which according to legend were men turned to stone for playing the Cornish sport of hurling on the Sabbath. Also within easy walking distance of the village is the **Cheesewring**, a strange granite formation reminiscent of a cheese press. Local folklore tells that it was home to a druid who provided thirsty passers-by with refreshment from a golden chalice that never ran dry.

7 BOLVENTOR

Situated at the heart of the moor, this tiny scenic hamlet is home to the old coaching inn immortalised in Daphne du Maurier's romantic novel *Jamaica Inn*. Sitting in the courtyard, supping a quiet pint, it is easy to see how du Maurier was inspired by the wild, windswept landscapes all around. The inn also houses a small **Smugglers' Museum**.

8 BODMIN MOOR AND DOZMARY POOL

The stillness of the bleak open moorland enfolds you in a blanket of silence as you turn off the A30. Although **Bodmin Moor** is comparatively small, the open, gently curving nature of the landscape, combined with the relative lack of features, creates a surprising sense of scale, remoteness and desolation. The quiet, brooding lake of **Dozmary Pool** lies in one of the most remote parts of the moor. It is here that Sir Bedevere is reputed to have thrown Excalibur, sword of King Arthur, as Arthur lay dying from wounds inflicted by his wicked nephew Mordred. A white hand is said to have arisen from the lake to take it to its depths.

Folklore also has it that Dozmary Pool is a bottomless lake (although it completely dried up during a drought in 1869), which the ghost of the infamous Cornish villain Jan Tregeagle was forced to empty with a leaky limpet shell as punishment for his wicked ways. Even today, there are those who believe the sound of the wind is Tregeagle moaning as demons chase him across the moor.

WARLEGGAN'S MAD MINISTER

A detour to Warleggan's squat little church recalls the intriguing story of the eccentric Reverend Frederick Densham. As the story goes, on taking up his post in this lonely moorland hamlet in 1931, the minister surrounded the rectory with barbed wire, patrolled the grounds with a pack of dogs and fitted the doors and windows with locks and bolts in order to alienate his parishioners. The villagers stayed away, and one entry in the register reads 'No fog. No wind. No rain. No congregation.' In response, the minister fashioned his own congregation from cardboard and preached undisturbed!

9 BLISLAND AND ST BREWARD

The pretty village of **Blisland** with its manor house, inn and old cottages set around a village green was much-loved by the poet John Betjeman. The parish church is mostly Norman with some 15th-century additions, and it features a beautiful colourful rood screen. Neighbouring **St Breward** is known for its granite quarries, and its stone has been used for national landmarks such as London's Tower Bridge. The church tower here, soaring to some 230m (750ft) above sea level, is the highest in Cornwall. The surrounding area is rich in reminders of past inhabitants with an ancient clapper bridge over the River De Lank and several prehistoric hut and stone circles within easy walking distance. Among them is the impressive **King Arthur's Hall**, a rectangular enclosure edged with upright stones. The site in fact has nothing to do with King Arthur but earned its name from the stones, which have the appearance of chairbacks.

Clockwise from far left: Golitha Falls; walkers, near Boscastle; Rough Tor

10 ROUGH TOR

The prominent heap of rocks known as Rough Tor forms the second-highest summit on Bodmin Moor, and the walk to its peak rewards the energetic with far-reaching views. Near the footbridge leading to the tor is a monument to 18-year-old Charlotte Dymond, who was murdered on the moor by her beau, crippled farm hand Matthew Weeks *(see p19)*.

*Continue north on unclassified roads to Watergate and turn right after the village to the car park for **Rough Tor**.* 10

11 BOSCASTLE

This stunning village clings to the side of the beautiful Valency Valley at the mouth of a natural harbour. It's a place to explore the pretty streets with their craft shops and higgledy-piggledy cottages, pay a visit to the intriguing **Museum of Witchcraft** and then drink in the atmosphere at one of the characterful old inns. Novelist Thomas Hardy met his wife, Emma, here and much of his novel *A Pair of Blue Eyes* is set in Boscastle. A lovely walk up the valley leads to **St Juliot Church**, which was restored by Hardy when he was working as an architect.

As you ramble around Boscastle's quiet streets it's difficult to imagine the horrendous flash floods that hit the village in August 2004. Although many homes and businesses suffered severe damage, most have now been fully rebuilt. The tourist information centre shows news footage from the fateful day.

*Drive north west to Camelford, turn left on the A39 then right soon after onto the B3266 to **Boscastle**.* 11

*Head west on the B3263 to **Tintagel**.*
→ • • • • • • • • • • 12

○ Head out of Tintagel on the
• B3263 and turn right onto
• unclassified roads to the
• B3314. Turn right, then after
• about 2 miles turn right
• again onto the unclassified
• road through Port Gaverne
• to *Port Isaac*. Continue on
⑬ the same road to *Port Quin*.

○ From Port Quin head
• south and take the
• unclassified roads
• through Polzeath and
• Trebetherick to *Rock*.
⑭ Visit *Padstow* by ferry.

12 TINTAGEL

To fully appreciate the atmosphere of King Arthur's legendary birthplace, climb the steps to ruined **Tintagel Castle**, perched high above the sea, and let your imagination run riot as the wind buffets you and the salt-spray flies in your face. From here, it's easy to visualise the stories of the gallant Knights of the Round Table and the cave beneath the castle where the magician Merlin lived. Back in the village there are a whole host of attractions given over to the legend, as well as the **Tintagel Old Post Office**, a tiny medieval manor house owned by the National Trust.

THE CAMEL TRAIL

This scenic cycle/walking route follows the disused railway alongside the River Camel from Padstow to Poley's Bridge on Bodmin Moor, via Wadebridge and Bodmin. The railway originally formed the final leg of the Atlantic Coast Express line from London's Waterloo and was immortalised in John Betjeman's poem *Cornwall* as 'the most beautiful train journey I know'. Bikes can be rented from several hire shops along the trail, including Bridge Bike Hire in Wadebridge and Padstow Cycle Hire in Padstow.

Clockwise from below: Tintagel Castle; boat, Port Isaac; fishing boats, Port Isaac; harbour, Padstow

13 PORT ISAAC AND PORT QUIN

Port Isaac is a lovely old fishing village full of character, with narrow streets – such as the aptly named Squeeze-ee-belly Alley – an inn and closely packed cottages. A twisting lane leads out of the village to **Port Quin**, a tiny hamlet that suffered greatly when the railways stole the slate trade from its once bustling quay. Its demise was so swift that outsiders were led to believe the entire population had been swept away in a great storm. Nearby, at **Pentire Point**, there are scenic headland walks once frequented by John Betjeman.

14 ROCK AND PADSTOW

Boasting wide, beautiful stretches of sand, the former fishing village of **Rock** is beloved by artists and yachtsmen and is now a major watersports centre. From the village you can walk across the golf course to **St Enodoc Church** where John Betjeman is buried *(see right)*.

Just across the Camel Estuary lies the scenic seaside town of **Padstow**. Since parking is difficult and it's quite a detour by road, abandon the car in Rock and take the ferry across. Padstow is famous for Rick Stein's award-wining **Seafood Restaurant**, which overlooks the harbour, and also for its colourful May Day 'Obby 'Oss Festival, when villagers follow the 'oss along the narrow streets and in and out of houses. Wander round the Old Quarter with its meandering streets and visit the **National Lobster Hatchery**, a marine conservation centre explaining how scientists are working to preserve the Cornish fishing tradition. Towering above the village is **Prideaux Place**, an Elizabethan gem filled with fine furniture, superb plasterwork and paintings, including a mid-18th-century portrait of Humphrey Prideaux by the Italian artist Rosalba Carriera. The artist hid a love letter to Humphrey in the canvas, but sadly he never discovered the letter or knew of her affections.

POETIC INSPIRATION

From childhood holidays spent at Trebetherick on the Camel Estuary, poet laureate Sir John Betjeman developed a deep connection to this part of Cornwall, lovingly evoking its landscape in *Old Friends*, *Summoned by Bells* and *Seaside Golf*. On summer evenings, recitals of his poems are held on Brae Hill, overlooking **St Enodoc Church** where he is buried. For a glimpse of his personal artefacts, visit the **Betjeman Centre**, housed in the old railway station at Wadebridge.

15 PENCARROW HOUSE AND GARDENS

This fine historic house, still very much lived in and loved by its present owners, contains a superb collection of pictures, furniture, porcelain and a number of antique dolls. Spring is a particularly lovely time to visit when the azaleas, camellias and rhododendrons in the 20-ha gardens (50 acres) are in bloom.

*From Rock, continue east on unclassified roads to the B3314 and turn right. Cross the A39 and continue on the A389 and follow signs left to **Pencarrow House and Gardens**.* **15**

*Drive back to the A389 and turn left to return to **Bodmin**.*

 **1**

WITH MORE TIME

With an extra day, you can add on a fabulous loop to visit the extraordinary **Eden Project** *(left)* near St Austell. The huge biomes here – the largest conservatories in the world – tell the story of man's relationship with plants and celebrate the diversity of earth's flora. You can wander among olive groves and citrus trees, marvel at tropical orchids and cocoa plants or explore the outdoor gardens planted with tea, hemp, bamboo and tobacco. A short drive further south are the **Lost Gardens of Heligan**, which have been beautifully restored after 70 years of neglect.

Beneath Dartmoor's craggy heights

Dotted with mysterious standing stones and bisected by sparkling streams, the bracken-covered expanse of Dartmoor forms southern England's last great wilderness. Here seekers of solitude can explore more than 600 miles of public footpaths across some of the loneliest tracts in England. There is often no human life for miles: just Dartmoor ponies grazing freely and birds of prey circling overhead. On the western fringes of the moor lies the tranquil Tamar Valley, where a river flows through a landscape scattered with ruined chimneys and abandoned quays that hark back to an era when this was one of England's richest mining regions.

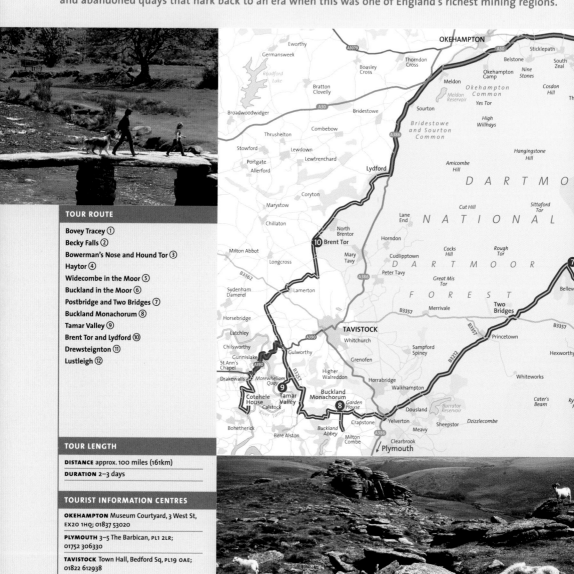

TOUR ROUTE

Bovey Tracey ①
Becky Falls ②
Bowerman's Nose and Hound Tor ③
Haytor ④
Widecombe in the Moor ⑤
Buckland in the Moor ⑥
Postbridge and Two Bridges ⑦
Buckland Monachorum ⑧
Tamar Valley ⑨
Brent Tor and Lydford ⑩
Drewsteignton ⑪
Lustleigh ⑫

TOUR LENGTH

DISTANCE approx. 100 miles (161km)
DURATION 2–3 days

TOURIST INFORMATION CENTRES

OKEHAMPTON Museum Courtyard, 3 West St, EX20 1HQ; 01837 53020

PLYMOUTH 3–5 The Barbican, PL1 2LR; 01752 306330

TAVISTOCK Town Hall, Bedford Sq, PL19 0AE; 01822 612938

1 BOVEY TRACEY

The River Bovey meanders right through this friendly old market town on Dartmoor's eastern edge. On its banks is the picturesque **Riverside Mill**, showcasing the work of more than 230 members of the Devon Guild of Craftsmen. More crafts await at the **Cardew Teapottery**, where you can see a variety of teapots being handcrafted, and at the **House of Marbles**, home to all manner of glass and marbles, complete with a shop, museum and regular glass-blowing demonstrations.

Bovey's most famous son was the wicked William de Tracey, one of the knights who murdered Thomas à Becket at Canterbury Cathedral in 1170. As penance, he built Bovey's **church**, dedicated to the saint, which houses a beautiful rood screen. Just outside the town is **Parke**, administrative headquarters of the Dartmoor National Park, from where you can enjoy some excellent woodland and riverside walks.

From Bovey Tracey take the
B3387 west and turn right
after half a mile onto unclassified roads to *Becky Falls*. ②

2 BECKY FALLS

A choice of trails through this lovely woodland park follow the picturesque Becka Brook as it tumbles 21m (70ft) down a series of giant boulders. It is the perfect spot for a picnic and a good place to get up close to some of Dartmoor's more reserved residents, including Dartmoor ponies and rescued birds of prey.

Continue north west past
Manaton and turn left onto
the unclassified road heading
south past *Bowerman's Nose*
on your left. Continue south
on this road to the *Hound
Tor* car park from where
you can walk to both tors. ③

3 BOWERMAN'S NOSE AND HOUND TOR

Eroded by wind and rain into strange shapes, these rocky outcrops are associated with a plethora of myths. **Bowerman's Nose** is the most intriguing, resembling a human head in profile. The most popular legend has it that the bowerman (hunter) disturbed a secret gathering of witches, who then petrified him and his hounds (of **Hound Tor** fame). Tales such as this inspired Sir Conan Doyle's story *Hound of the Baskervilles* in 1902. Whether these tales have any truth or not, it's an isolated spot, indescribably bleak even on the sunniest day. South east of Hound Tor are the ruins of a medieval village, well worth the extra walk.

Continue south on the
same road to the B3387,
then turn left to *Haytor*.
→ • • • • • • • • • • • ④

⊕ *Return west on the B3387*
  to **Widecombe**
⑤ *in the Moor.*

4 HAYTOR

Its accessible location close to the road makes Haytor arguably the most visited of Dartmoor's tors. Climb to the top of this rugged rockpile for views that stretch as far as the coast on a clear day. Behind the tor you can see evidence of the old railway along which sturdy Dartmoor ponies used to haul granite from the nearby quarries to then be used in famous structures such as London Bridge. The National Park Information Centre in the lower car park on the main road stocks a good selection of leaflets and maps detailing further walks in the vicinity.

5 WIDECOMBE IN THE MOOR

Widecombe's grand 14th-century **church** has been dubbed the 'cathedral of the moor' and it is an impressive sight as you drop down into the village from the moorland above. The village makes for a pleasant stopping off point to wander the pretty streets lined with whitewashed houses and tearooms, and enjoy a hearty lunch at one of the two pubs. Widecombe is best known for its annual fair in September, which includes such traditional country events as sheep shearing, bale tossing and a tug of war.

⊕ *Take the unclassified*
  roads south to **Buckland**
⑥ *in the Moor.*

Clockwise from far left:
Haytor; church, Widecombe
in the Moor; mural,
Buckland Abbey; cottages,
Buckland in the Moor

6 BUCKLAND IN THE MOOR

Tucked away down a maze of country lanes, this miniscule hamlet is famous for its picture-book thatched cottages, which have appeared on countless chocolate boxes and calendars. Look out for the clock on the church tower, which has the words 'MY DEAR MOTHER' instead of numbers on its face. The clock was a tribute by the local lord of the manor, William Whitley, to his mother on her death in the 1930s. He also inscribed two tablets on the summit of nearby **Buckland Beacon** with the words of the Ten Commandments. The lettering is much weathered but the views alone are worth the climb.

7 POSTBRIDGE AND TWO BRIDGES

The best preserved of Dartmoor's 30 or so clapper bridges crosses the East Dart at **Postbridge**. It is a popular spot, with a useful visitor information centre, so try to visit early or late to fully appreciate the lovely setting. From here the road winds across the lonely sheep-studded moor, through **Two Bridges** where residents tell of a phantom pair of 'hairy hands' that have forced many drivers off the road. The area has long been feared by locals.

8 BUCKLAND MONACHORUM

One of England's best-loved gardens awaits in this photogenic village nestling on the edge of Dartmoor. The **Garden House** is renowned for the naturalistic style of its 3ha (8 acres) including a stunning walled garden set around the ruins of a medieval vicarage. Just outside the village is **Buckland Abbey**, a former Cistercian abbey, famed as the home of Sir Francis Drake. The house contains some fascinating exhibits of the great explorer's colourful exploits, including Drake's drum, which, it is said, will beat of its own accord to summon the great man should England ever need his help. The village church contains a tribute to the generations of Drakes who lived here; look out for the carving of Drake's ship, the *Golden Hind*, on the family pew.

DARTMOOR 'LETTERBOXES'

From small beginnings in 1854, the pursuit of 'letterboxing' has escalated to enormous proportions. Today, there are more than 3,000 'letterboxes' of all shapes and sizes hidden across the moor. Each contains a rubber stamp pertinent to the location, which dedicated followers can use to stamp their own books or cards as proof of their visit. The boxes are almost impossible to find without some inside knowledge, but you can purchase clue sheets and there are also some books available.

*Drive on unclassified roads
north west to Postbridge,
then turn left on the B3212
to **Two Bridges**.*

*Take the B3212 south west
to Yelverton. Cross the
A386 and continue west on
unclassified roads to
Buckland Monachorum.*

*Continue west to the B3257
and turn right. After about
2 miles, turn left to
Morwhellam Quay. Return
to the B3257 and turn left.
Turn left again onto the
A390 and just past
Gunnislake turn left and
follow the unclassified roads
for 4 miles to **Cotehele**.*

Clockwise from above:
aqueduct, Tamar Valley;
White Lady Waterfall,
Lydford; Castle Drogo,
Drewsteignton; Cotehele,
Tamar Valley

*From Cotehele, return to
the A390 and turn right.
At Gulworthy turn left
and follow the unclassified
roads across the B3362
to **Brent Tor** car park just
south of North Brentor.
Continue north east
to **Lydford**.*

→ • • • • • • • • • • ⑩

9 TAMAR VALLEY

It is hard to imagine, but during its mining heyday this tranquil valley was one of the busiest waterways in the country and the quaysides bristled with ships' masts. The museum village of **Morwhellam Quay** gives you the opportunity to step back in time and experience what it must have been like. Costumed staff accompany you round the riverside trams, miners' cottages and underground into the old copper mine. Across the river at Cotehele Quay, the restored sailing barge *Shamrock* is moored alongside the **Cotehele Quay Museum**, which tells the story of the River Tamar. Set in beautiful terraced gardens above the quay is the medieval stately home of **Cotehele**, which includes a magnificent Great Hall and some fine tapestries.

A WALK THROUGH HISTORY

A wealth of ancient remains – many of which are accessible only on foot – are testimony to more than 4,500 years of human habitation on Dartmoor. Just south of Okehampton, a half-mile climb leads up onto the moors from Belstone Church to the atmospheric **Nine Stones** stone circle, which despite its name is made up of 11 stones out of the original 40 or so that must have been here. Another memorable climb is from Sheepstor to **Drizzlecombe**, where a collection of standing stones, cairns, stone circles and long rows are sited in classic moorland surroundings.

If you're after a more substantial trek, the circular **Dartmoor Way** traces a 90-mile route linking Dartmoor's historic small towns and villages including Okehampton, Bovey Tracey and Princetown, taking in wild moorland scenery, clapper bridges and tors along the way. Alternatively you can explore the **Two Moors Way**, which begins in Ivybridge before traversing some of the remotest sections of the moor en route to Exmoor, passing prehistoric stones, abandoned mine buildings and a section of disused tramway.

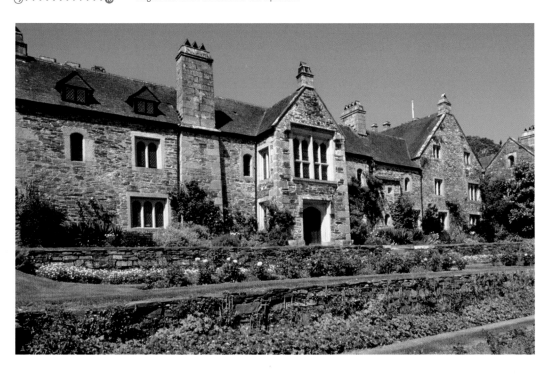

10 BRENT TOR AND LYDFORD

On the way to Lydford, stop off at **Brent Tor** and climb the footpath to the summit, where the squat little **Church of St Michael** surveys the lonely moorland below. Though sometimes shrouded in cloud, the views on a clear day are outstanding and the stillness is broken only by the cries of the birds wheeling overhead.

Lydford's main claim to fame is its spectacular wooded gorge, home in the 17th century to a band of outlaws whose exploits are recalled in Charles Kingsley's *Westward Ho!* Follow the circular path from the National Trust centre south to the impressive 27-m **White Lady Waterfall** (90ft) and **Devil's Cauldron**, where the thundering water hisses and spits through a series of whirlpools. Lydford itself is a quiet little place, dominated by its forbidding **castle**, once a prison. Pay a visit to the lovely **church**, with its carved pews and peaceful churchyard. For centuries, Dartmoor's dead were brought down from the moor along the ancient Lych Way to be buried here.

11 DREWSTEIGNTON

Thatched cottages and a medieval granite church cluster round the green in this picturesque hilltop village with its inviting pub. From the village, a footpath leads down to Fingle Bridge, which spans the River Teign in an idyllic setting. Perched on a rocky crag high above the river, with marvellous views, is **Castle Drogo**; behind its austere exterior lies a veritable treasure-trove of rich furnishings and tapestries.

12 LUSTLEIGH

This is one of Dartmoor's loveliest villages with cottages and a thatched pub grouped around a pretty 13th-century church. It is a perfect stopping-off point to enjoy a traditional Devonshire cream tea. A short walk across the clapper bridge leads to the hamlet of **Wreyland**, where thatched cottages are set in exquisite gardens.

Continue through Lydford to the A386 and turn left, then turn right onto the A30. After about 8 miles, turn right onto the A382 then left on unclassified roads to **Drewsteignton**. ⑪

Head west on the unclassified road past Castle Drogo to the A382. Cross over the A382 and continue on unclassified roads and the B2206 through Chagford and North Bovey to **Lustleigh**. ⑫

Drive north east half a mile and turn right on the A382 to return to **Bovey Tracey**.
← • • • • • • • • • • • ❶

WITH MORE TIME

South of Dartmoor is **Plymouth**, a town steeped in maritime history. Among its attractions are the Hoe where Sir Francis Drake *(left)* finished his game of bowls before confronting the Spanish Armada; the historic Barbican quarter from where the Pilgrim Fathers set sail to America; and the excellent Plymouth Dome, which recounts Plymouth's seafaring past. Regular boat trips from the Barbican take in the waterfront sights, including the warships and submarines on the River Tamar and the Tudor Mount Edgcumbe House set in a vast country park.

The English Riviera and the sleepy South Hams

Chic, cosmopolitan Torquay lies at the northern end of the 'English Riviera', the cluster of seaside resorts around Tor Bay. Each has its own character: from nautical Brixham and kiss-me-quick Paignton to Torquay, the undisputed 'queen', with her luxury hotels and sparkling marina. From here, wind south into the tranquil, rural landscape of the South Hams where patchwork fields drop down to estuaries thronged with boats.

TOUR ROUTE

Torquay ①
Brixham ②
Coleton Fishacre ③
Dartmouth ④
Start Bay ⑤
Start Point ⑥
Kingsbridge and Salcombe ⑦
Overbeck's Museum and Garden ⑧
Bigbury-on-Sea and Burgh Island ⑨
Dittisham ⑩
Totnes ⑪
Berry Pomeroy Castle ⑫

TOUR LENGTH

DISTANCE approx. 95 miles (150 km)
DURATION 2–3 days

TOURIST INFORMATION CENTRES

DARTMOUTH The Engine House, Mayor's Ave, TQ6 9YY; 01803 834224

EXETER Civic Centre, Dix's Field, EX1 1RQ; 01392 265700

TORQUAY The Tourist Centre, Vaughan Parade, TQ2 5JG; 0870 70 70 010

Miles 0 ———————— 5
Kms 0 ———————— 5

Clockwise from far left:
harbour, Torquay; Blackpool
Sands, Start Bay; Golden
Hind, Brixham; coastal
path, Hope Cove

1 TORQUAY

With its villa-clad hillsides, palm-lined promenades and millionaires' yachts bobbing in the marina, Torquay is a slice of the continent in England's south west. The old harbour brims with shops and lively waterfront cafes and has a particularly Mediterranean feel. Here you'll find **Living Coasts**, an aquatic attraction devoted to the conservation of coastal flora and fauna. A few minutes north of the harbour, **Torquay Museum** houses a gallery devoted to the crime writer Agatha Christie, one of Torquay's most famous residents. It also includes prehistoric archaeological finds from **Kents Cavern**, one mile out of town, which is open for underground tours.

A stroll west along the seafront brings you to Torquay's oldest building, **Torre Abbey**, dating from 1196, and its adjacent medieval Spanish Barn that is named after the Armada prisoners held here in 1588. Although both are closed for refurbishment until 2008, you can still walk around the exotic gardens, complete with Victorian palmhouse. The abbey lies just inland from Torquay's largest and most popular beach, the gently sloping **Torre Abbey Sands**, one of 20 beaches along Tor Bay's 22 miles of coast. If you prefer to escape the crowds, there are plenty of other sunspots, including the picturesque **Meadfoot Beach** with its views of Thatcher Rock.

Also worth a visit is chocolate-box-pretty **Cockington**, a thatched village nestled somewhat incongruously in Torquay's western suburbs. Visit the craft workshops at **Cockington Court** or picnic in the landscaped grounds, which feature lakes and woodland walks.

*From Torquay's seafront
follow the A379/
A3022 to **Brixham**.*

2 BRIXHAM

This intimate little town was once one of Britain's largest fishing ports, and the sea remains its lifeblood. Follow the quayside past the fish stalls and climb aboard the reconstructed *Golden Hind* to experience the cramped conditions faced by Sir Francis Drake when he circumnavigated the world between 1577 and 1580. Then, find out more about the town's seafaring past at the **Brixham Heritage Museum**. For panoramic sea views, take a walk east to **Berry Head**, where the clifftop lighthouse, at only 4.5m (15ft) tall, is both the highest and shortest in Britain.

*Return on the A3022 to the
junction with the A379 and
turn left. Soon after, turn
left onto the B3205 then
left again on unclassified
roads following signs to
Coleton Fishacre.*

⊕ *Return to the B3205 and turn left towards Kingswear. Remain on this road following signs for the Lower Ferry to* **④** *cross to* **Dartmouth**.

⊕ *Head south on the B3205 and turn left on the A379 to* **Start Bay** *via Stoke Fleming and then* **⑤** *continue to Torcross.*

From Torcross' seafront proceed on unclassified roads via Hallsands to **Start Point.**

→ • • • • • • • • • ⑥

Clockwise from below left: Dartmouth; lighthouse, Start Point; Salcombe castle; pub sign, Salcombe

3 COLETON FISHACRE

Opera lovers and garden enthusiasts will both enjoy a visit to this stunning seaside home of the famous operatic D'Oyly Carte family. As you wander round the beautiful gardens, familiar Gilbert and Sullivan melodies spill from the windows of the Arts and Crafts-styled house. Below, the garden plunges down into a steeply wooded coombe to the cliff's edge and is magnificent in spring when the camellias, rhododendrons and magnolias are a blaze of colour.

4 DARTMOUTH

The car ferry from Kingswear to Dartmouth takes only a few minutes, so have your camera at the ready as you cross the Dart Estuary to reach this picturesque town clinging to the hillside. Wander round the old streets and along the historic cobbled quayside lined with elegant 18th-century houses to **Bayard's Cove**, where the Pilgrim Fathers repaired their ships before hoisting sail to the New World. From here it's a 20-minute walk south along the river to **Dartmouth Castle**, which, together with Kingswear Castle on the opposite bank, guards the entrance to the estuary. To best appreciate the town's magical setting, join a scenic boat cruise or take a trip on the **Dart Valley Railway**, which runs north to the resort of Paignton. Look out for the impressive Britannia Royal Naval College, dominating the skyline above Dartmouth.

THE CHRISTIE CONNECTION

Agatha Christie (previously Agatha Mary Clarissa Miller) was born in Torquay in 1890 and lived much of her life in the area. Fans of her crime novels will recognise many of the places woven into her stories including Kents Cavern, setting for Hempsley Cavern in *The Man in the Brown Suit*, and Torquay's Imperial Hotel – the Majestic in *The Body in the Library*. Plans are afoot to open a Christie visitor centre, but in the meantime you can follow the **Christie Mile** walk along the seafront, which takes in buildings and sites associated with the writer including the Torquay Museum *(see p31)*. A leaflet is available from local tourist information centres.

5 START BAY

The scenic A379 sweeps south from Dartmouth to join the sea at the pretty village of **Stoke Fleming** overlooking Start Bay. One mile south is **Blackpool Sands**, one of the best beaches in the country with clean, clear water. Further on, the road winds down to **Slapton Sands**, a three-mile sand and shingle bar used by the Allied Troops as a practice area for the D-Day landings in World War II. Tragically, they were attacked by an enemy E-boat and more than 600 soldiers were killed. A memorial at **Torcross**, alongside the Sherman tank recovered from the sea, commemorates their lives. Behind Slapton Sands, the freshwater lake at **Slapton Ley National Nature Reserve** is a prime spot for birdwatching.

6 START POINT

As you stand at Start Point, pummelled by the wind, with the waves thundering below, it is easy to appreciate how the treacherous seas around this exposed peninsula have claimed so many lives. In the past, captured pirates were hung in chains here as a warning to their fellow brigands. Nowadays, the only warning is the reassuring beam from the lighthouse, open to visitors, which affords stunning views. A further reminder of the power of the sea can be found a few miles north at **Hallsands**. Today, only a hotel and a few cottages remain of this once-thriving fishing community, which collapsed into the sea one stormy night in 1917. Many of the now-ruined houses are still in evidence.

7 KINGSBRIDGE AND SALCOMBE

The bustling market town of **Kingsbridge** lies in an attractive setting at the head of its tidal estuary. Handsome Tudor and Georgian houses characterise the town, in particular along steep, shop-lined Fore Street, which includes the colonnaded Shambles, once the market arcade. The **Cookworthy Museum** contains a number of fascinating photographs of the now-abandoned village of Hallsands *(see left)*.

The pretty riverside town of **Salcombe**, hugging a hillside three miles downstream, is a favourite destination with visiting yachtsmen. There is an array of chandlery shops as well as a plethora of chic boutiques and restaurants, in addition to lovely estuary views.

*Head north west on unclassified roads through South Pool to Frogmore and turn left onto the A379 to **Kingsbridge**. From Kingsbridge turn south on unclassified roads to **Salcombe**. (Alternatively take the ferry from Kingsbridge in summer.)* **7**

*Take the ferry from Salcombe to South Sands (about one mile south) and walk up the steep hill to **Overbeck's Museum and Garden**. (Alternatively, follow the signs by car from Salcombe along the steep single track road.)*

 **8**

Head north on the A381
and turn left onto the
B3197, then turn left again
onto the A379. Before
Modbury take another
left onto the B3392 to
⑨ *Bigbury-on-Sea.*

COASTAL WALKS

The long-distance **South West Coast Path** traces
the same coast covered by this driving tour, so
there are opportunities aplenty to don your
hiking books and take to the paths. One of the
most strenuous, but exhilarating sections of
the path in this area is from Bolt Head, south
of Salcombe, west to Bolt Tail; the path
meanders along precipitous cliffs where gulls
and cormorants wheel and scream, and views,
on a clear day, reach as far as Burgh Island. For
a gentler – but equally beautiful – stroll, walk
north from the sandy beach at pretty Hope Cove
to Bantham beach via thatched Thurlestone
(below), with its natural arched rock.

*Return on the B3392 to the
A379 and cross over.
Continue on unclassified
roads through California
Cross to Harbertonford.
Turn right onto the A381
then left onto unclassified
roads through Cornworthy
to* Dittisham.

→ • • • • • • • • • • • ⑩

Clockwise from below:
Burgh Island; Totnes Castle;
River Dart, Totnes

8 OVERBECK'S MUSEUM AND GARDEN

This hidden gem is well worth a visit for the rather
bizarre legacy of eccentric scientist Otto Overbeck,
who lived here from 1928 to 1937. These include his
collections of shipbuilding tools and natural history
artefacts, as well as some of his inventions. Among
them is an electrical rejuvenator, patented in 1924, that
was supposed to extend human life to the age of 350.
The house is set in 2.5ha (6 acres) of tropical gardens
with fabulous vistas of the estuary.

9 BIGBURY-ON-SEA AND BURGH ISLAND

Deservedly popular for its acres of sandy beach,
Bigbury-on-Sea's star attraction is **Burgh Island**,
accessible on foot at low tide or by a giant sea tractor
when the tide is in. The island is dominated by its
extravagant Art-Deco hotel, which has attracted many
famous patrons including Agatha Christie, who set
several of her stories here. After climbing to the top of
the island, indulge in a cream tea at the hotel, or sup a
pint at the Pilchard Inn and drink in the views.

10 DITTISHAM

Narrow streets lined with stone and thatched cottages drop steeply to the River Dart in this atmospheric yachting village, featuring a lovely church. Ring the bell near the Ferry Boat Inn to summon the passenger ferry to **Greenway** across the river, to visit the gardens at the former country home of Agatha Christie. In the middle of the river you will see the Anchor Stone, where, legend has it, the unfaithful wives of the village were tied up as punishment.

11 TOTNES

Strategically located at the highest navigable limit and lowest crossing point of the River Dart, this ancient and virtually unspoiled hillside town has been an important settlement since Saxon times and is packed with archaeological remains. Today, Totnes is widely known for its diverse, creative community that gives the town quite a distinct atmosphere. The town boasts a particularly fine selection of wholefood shops, boutiques, secondhand bookstores and centres offering complimentary therapies. There's also a good range of arts and crafts on offer in the numerous galleries dotted around and at the local market held on Fridays and Saturdays throughout the year in the Civic Square.

Begin an exploration at the Old Steamer Quay, where the Dartmouth cruises put to shore. From here, Fore Street, lined with fine old merchants' houses, rises steeply. One house accommodates the **Elizabethan Museum** where items of local historical interest, including displays on Victorian mathematician Charles Babbage, inventor of the forerunner of the computer, are exhibited. Pass through the handsome medieval East Gate arch and turn right to the 11th-century **Guildhall**, where you can visit the old jail and see the table where Oliver Cromwell sat in 1646.

On the main High Street, look out for the columned arcades of Poultry Walk and the Butterwalk, which stand in sharp contrast to the modern façade of the **Civic Hall** opposite; the latter is the venue on Tuesdays during the summer for Totnes' Elizabethan market, where traders dress up in period costume. At the top of the hill the Norman **castle** boasts one of the best-preserved keeps in the country.

12 BERRY POMEROY CASTLE

Perched high above a romantic, wooded gorge, Berry Pomeroy is unusual in consisting of two sets of ruins, with the remains of an Elizabethan mansion set inside the old castle walls. It is also reputed to be one of the most haunted places in Britain. According to legend, the White Lady is the spirit of Margaret Pomeroy, starved to death here by her sister Eleanor, and it is said that all who see her meet an untimely end.

Return west to Cornworthy and continue on unclassified roads via Tuckenhay to the A381. Turn right and then turn right again onto the A385 and continue to **Totnes**.

Leave Totnes heading east on the A385. Just out of town turn left to Berry Pomeroy and follow signs to **Berry Pomeroy Castle**.

Travel east on unclassified roads to the A380. Continue across, heading east, then turn left onto the A3022 and then right on the A379 to return to **Torquay**.

WITH MORE TIME

The historic city of **Exeter**, with its timbered buildings and cobbled streets, makes for an absorbing day out. Begin at the medieval cathedral *(left)*, which has a magnificent fan-vaulted ceiling and carved Bishop's Throne, then wander round the close and explore the shops and 14th-century Guildhall on the High Street. Just north are the trendy boutiques and wine bars of Gandy Street and the Royal Albert Memorial Museum and Art Gallery, worth a visit for its eclectic displays. Finish at the old quayside, which buzzes with stylish shops and restaurants.

Rural backwaters of North Devon

Far from the honeypots of Devon's south and the county's two alluring national parks, this tranquil enclave dotted with historic market towns and little-known attractions is, for many, the quintessential Devon. Inland, steep, narrow lanes wind through a rural landscape characterised by undulating hills, ancient villages and isolated farmsteads. To the north lies Devon's most spectacular sweep of coast – a string of rugged cliffs eroded by the ferocious sea and interspersed with wide sandy beaches – where windswept footpaths, historic ports and time-forgotten villages invite exploration far off the beaten track.

TOUR ROUTE

Barnstaple ①
Tapeley Park ②
Bideford ③
Appledore ④
Buck's Mills and Clovelly ⑤
Hartland Point ⑥
Great Torrington ⑦
Cobbaton Combat Collection ⑧
Arlington Court ⑨
Ilfracombe ⑩
Woolacombe ⑪
Marwood Hill Gardens ⑫

TOUR LENGTH

DISTANCE approx. 115 miles (185km)

DURATION 2–3 days

TOURIST INFORMATION CENTRES

BARNSTAPLE Museum of North Devon, The Square, EX32 8LN; 01271 375000

BIDEFORD Victoria Park, The Quay, EX39 2QQ; 01237 477676

ILFRACOMBE The Landmark, The Seafront, EX34 9BX; 01271 863001

Clockwise from far left:
countryside, near Buck's
Mills; harbour, Clovelly;
Arlington Court; cottage,
Buck's Mills

1 BARNSTAPLE

Many fine buildings remain from the days when
Barnstaple was a prosperous port, including the
colonnaded Queen Anne's Walk on the old quayside.
Built as a merchants' exchange, it now houses the
Barnstaple Heritage Centre, which explores the key
events in Barnstaple's history through a wealth of
audio-visual and interactive displays. From here, a
riverside walk follows part of the long-distance Tarka
Trail *(see p38)* under the 13th-century Long Bridge to the
Museum of Barnstaple and North Devon, where there's an
impressive display of 18th-century North Devon pottery.
   Barnstaple's huge covered **Pannier Market** (daily
except Sundays) is the largest market in Devon, well
worth a visit as much for its grand wrought iron
architecture as for the range of crafts and produce for
sale. Its name derives from the wicker baskets once
used to carry produce to the market in the 19th
century. **Butcher's Row**, nearby, is a series of archways
with brightly coloured canopies, built exclusively to
house butchers' shops. Many still trade here today
alongside fishmongers, delicatessens and other food
shops. Away from the market bustle, the **Penrose
Almshouses** in Litchdon Street are also worth seeking
out. Built in 1634 to house the poor of the town and
still fulfiling their original purpose, an atmosphere of
gentle calm pervades here.

*Head south west out of
Barnstaple on the B3125 to
join the B3233 heading
west. Shortly after Instow
turn left to **Tapeley Park**.* ②

2 TAPELEY PARK

Tapeley's 8-ha gardens (20 acres) descend from a
Georgian mansion in a series of Italianate terraces,
brimming with colours and aromas, and affording
stunning views over the Torridge Estuary below. The
gardens have been restored over recent years and
contain many rare and tender species including the
oldest *Thuja plicata* trees in England, which are set
around a tranquil lake.

*Return to the B3233,
turn left and continue
to **Bideford**.*
③

Clockwise from above:
quay, Bideford; lighthouse,
Hartland Point; Clovelly

*Follow the
A386 north to
4 Appledore.*

THE TARKA TRAIL

Henry Williamson's famous adventures of an otter cub born on the banks of the River Torridge infuse this part of North Devon. Many of the places that feature in his evocative novel *Tarka the Otter* (1927) remain remarkably unchanged and can be seen on the **Tarka Trail**, a 180-mile waymarked foot and cycle path that tracks the otter's wanderings between the valleys of the Taw and Torridge. Leaflets covering certain sections of the trail are available from local tourist offices. The book has also given its name to the **Tarka Line**, the picturesque rail route that follows the River Taw south east from Barnstaple to Exeter.

3 BIDEFORD

Life in Bideford still centres around the old quayside, where vessels laden with tobacco from the New World once docked and from where valiant little ships set sail to challenge the Spanish Armada in 1588. From the quay, the ancient Long Bridge straddles the Torridge Estuary across to the Royal Hotel, where Charles Kingsley penned much of his famous novel *Westward Ho!* Another of Bideford's famous sons was naval commander Sir Richard Grenville, the man who brought back one of the first native Americans ever to walk on English soil, who was baptised at Bideford church in 1585. Grenville's portrait and information on his various exploits can be found at the **Burton Art Gallery and Museum**, situated adjacent to Victoria Park close to the bridge. Behind the park, streets of fine merchants' houses climb the steep hillside to the splendid **Market Hall**, which houses the Pannier Market on Tuesdays and Saturdays.

4 APPLEDORE

A maze of narrow lanes lined with sturdy, flower-bedecked fishermen's cottages rise steeply from Appledore's old quay. Shipbuilding still continues here, though today this pretty village is more of a haunt for visiting yachtsmen and tourists who come to browse in the galleries and craft shops, or to sample the tantalisingly fresh seafood. You can soak up Appledore's seafaring past at the **North Devon Maritime Museum**, where assorted nautical artefacts range from cannons to World War II memorabilia.

Travel south west on unclassified roads through Abbotsham to join the A39. Turn right and continue about 5 miles to the right-hand turning to Buck's Mill. Rejoin the A39 and turn right, then turn right again on the B3237 to Clovelly.

5

5 BUCK'S MILLS AND CLOVELLY

A steep, hidden lane through a beautiful wooded valley leads to the tiny village of **Buck's Mills**, which clings to a hillside above the sea. You have to park at the top of the village and walk down the sloping main street lined with traditional whitewashed cottages to the stony beach, with its old limekiln.

Along the coast is Buck's more famous neighbour, Clovelly (no cars are allowed here either). It is an impossibly pretty place: flower-festooned cottages flank the steep cobbled main street, known as Up-a-long or Down-a-long depending on which way you're going. At the bottom is the sheltered harbour from where there are good views of the village rising steeply above. Charles Kingsley went to school here when his father was rector at the church, and it was Clovelly that inspired him to write his enduring classic *The Water Babies*. The **Kingsley Museum** explores the writer's association with the village. If you don't fancy the uphill haul back to your car, a Land Rover service operates from the Red Lion pub.

6 HARTLAND POINT

The relentless pounding of the sea on this wild stretch of coastline has undermined the rocks beneath **Hartland Point's** sturdy lighthouse to such an extent that a sea wall had to be built to protect it from further damage. From here, the South West Coast Path scrambles south over the jagged cliffs, popular with abseilers, to **Hartland Quay** on what is one of the most rewarding coastal walks in England. Despite being exposed to the full fury of the Atlantic, this was once a busy quay until it was swept away in 1887. The old quayside buildings are house a hotel and **The Hartland Quay Museum** displaying salvage from the ships that have foundered here over the centuries. Twenty minutes walk south along the coast brings you to **Spekes Mill Mouth Waterfall** where a stream cascades down a sheer rock face to the sea.

Just inland, at the pretty hamlet of **Stoke**, the tower of **St Nectan's Church**, the tallest in Devon, warns ships of the perilous rocks on this stretch of coast. Inside is a painted wagon-roof ceiling and intricately carved 15th-century screen. Nearby, **Hartland Abbey** once housed the monks who worshipped at the church; today it is a historic home containing a superb collection of porcelain, paintings and furniture, all set in beautiful gardens with scenic walks leading down to the sea.

Return to the A39 and turn right to join the B3248 west to Hartland, then continue north on unclassified roads to Hartland Point. From here drive south on unclassified roads via Hartland Abbey to Stoke and Hartland Quay.

Return via Hartland and join the B3248 east. Turn left onto the A39 and right almost immediately onto unclassified roads through Buckland Brewer to join the A386 in to Great Torrington.

Take the B3227 north east and turn left after about 9 miles onto the unclassified road through Chittlehampton to the **Cobbaton Combat Collection**.

Continue north on unclassified roads through Swimbridge and Stoke Rivers to **Arlington Court**.

Drive north on unclassified roads through East Down to the A3123 and turn left. Shortly after, turn right to Berrynarbor. Continue north, turning left onto the A399 to Watermouth Bay. From here continue west on the A399 to **Ilfracombe**.

7 GREAT TORRINGTON

Strategically positioned above the River Torridge, it was at Great Torrington that one of the last great battles of the English Civil War took place in 1646. More than 17,000 troops fought in the streets and 200 royalist soldiers were blown up along with St Michael's Church, which was being used as a gunpowder store at the time. Costumed characters replay the events at the **Torrington 1646** museum, located on Castle Hill from where there are fabulous views of the River Torridge below.

Aside from its pretty main square and refurbished Pannier Market, Torrington is best known for the **Dartington Crystal Visitor Centre**, where you can take a tour and observe the stages of crystal production, and for the RHS **Rosemoor** garden with its impressive collection of more than 2,000 roses.

Clockwise from below:
Rosemoor, Great Torrington;
Croyde Bay

CATCHING THE PERFECT WAVE

Lashed by Atlantic rollers, North Devon boasts some of the best surfing beaches in England. Top of the list with experienced surfers is **Croyde Bay** *(below)*, where powerful waves have enticed some of the sport's top competitors including former British champion Richard Carter. **Westward Ho!, Woolacombe Bay** and nearby **Putsborough** are also popular surfing spots, while the gentler sloping beach at **Saunton Sands** is a favourite with beginners and longboarders. Boards, wetsuits and expert tuition are available at most beaches. For more information on surfing in the UK contact the British Surfing Association.

8 COBBATON COMBAT COLLECTION

One of Devon's most unlikely attractions awaits in the tiny farming community of Cobbaton. The Cobbaton Combat Collection is the work of Preston Isaac, who began amassing wartime memorabilia as a schoolboy. Today, his cluttered and ever-growing collection includes over 50 military vehicles and artillery pieces together with thousands of smaller items.

9 ARLINGTON COURT

The featureless exterior of Arlington Court belies the wealth of riches that lie within. Beautifully appointed rooms display the remarkable collection of Miss Rosalie Chichester, who lived here until 1949. Among the treasures are numerous model ships, more than 50 cabinets of shells and hundreds of snuff boxes and trinkets gathered on her travels round the world. Outside, a walk through attractive parkland leads to the stables, which house the National Trust's collection of some 50 horse-drawn carriages. Rides are available in the summer.

10 ILFRACOMBE

This popular resort has changed little since its Victorian heyday. On a rock above the pretty harbour, which is thronged with fishing boats and pleasure craft, stands the tiny **Chapel of St Nicholas**. Once a refuge for pilgrims travelling to Hartland Abbey, the church has shone a light from its window to guide boats into the harbour since the Middle Ages. On the seafront are the famous **Tunnel Beaches**, with four hand-carved tunnels leading through the cliff face to beaches and a tidal bathing pool. To the east, the rocky coastline is studded with sheltered inlets including the sandy cove of **Watermouth Bay** guarded by the imposing Victorian **Watermouth Castle**, now a family attraction with a theme park. Inland lies the picturesque village of **Berrynarbour**, with its quaint cottages and well-tended gardens, that nestles at the foot of the beautiful Sterridge Valley.

11 WOOLACOMBE

Woolacombe's wide sweep of sand is sprinkled with rock pools and scoured clean by Atlantic rollers, making it a popular choice with families and surfers alike. Follow the coastal footpath north to **Morte Point** and soak up the wild beauty of this glorious stretch of coastline with views extending to Lundy Island *(see below)*, 12 miles out to sea. Along the coast, the lighthouse at **Bull Point** warns of treacherous rocks where ships have come to grief. Further south the beaches at **Croyde** are a surfers' paradise *(see left)*. With its thatched cottages and tearooms, the village here still retains much of its old world charm.

12 MARWOOD HILL GARDENS

This 7-ha garden (18 acres) is built around three lakes with a range of trees, shrubs and herbaceous plants that guarantee colour all year round, from drifts of winter snowdrops to summer's vibrant hues. If you can, visit in the late spring when the waxy show of the rhododendrons and camellias is simply spectacular.

Follow the unclassified roads south west to join the B3343 and turn right to Woolacombe then drive south on unclassified roads to Croyde. ⑪

Take the B3231 south east to Braunton then follow unclassified roads east to Marwood Hill Gardens. ⑫

Travel south on unclassified roads to join the A361 to return to Barnstaple. ①

WITH MORE TIME

Take a day trip to tiny **Lundy Island** *(left)* on the *MS Oldenburg*, which sails from Ilfracombe and Bideford from March to October. This rocky outcrop, just three and a half miles long by half a mile wide and with a population of around 18, is a world apart, tranquil and unspoilt. Owned by the National Trust, it is home to a handful of houses, one shop, one pub and thousands of seabirds, including puffins, which can be sighted from April to May during mating season. It also offers plentiful opportunities for walking, climbing and snorkelling.

The magic of Exmoor

Straddling the boundary between Somerset and Devon, Exmoor is a wild, remote expanse of heather-clad moorland, deep wooded coombes sliced with sparkling streams and a spectacular coastline that is second to none. One of Britain's least discovered national parks, it spans 267 sq miles with over 620 miles of scenic footpaths and an astonishing diversity of flora and fauna, including shy Exmoor ponies and England's only herd of wild red deer. Landscape and literature are inextricably linked here, and the irresistibly romantic landscape has been the source of inspiration for many a literary masterpiece.

TOUR ROUTE

Dunster ①
Minehead ②
Selworthy ③
Porlock and Porlock Weir ④
Doone Country ⑤
Watersmeet ⑥
Lynmouth and Lynton ⑦
Valley of the Rocks and Woody Bay ⑧
Simonsbath ⑨
Exford and Withypool ⑩
Tarr Steps ⑪
Winsford ⑫
Dunkery Beacon ⑬

TOUR LENGTH

DISTANCE approx. 76 miles (122km)

DURATION 3 days

TOURIST INFORMATION CENTRES

LYNTON Town Hall, Lee Rd, EX35 6BT;
0845 660 3232

MINEHEAD 17 Friday St, TA24 5UB;
01643 702624

Clockwise from far left:
sheep, near Porlock; walker,
near Dunkery Beacon;
Dunster; cottage, Selworthy

Miles 0 —————————— 5
Kms 0 —————————— 5

1 DUNSTER

This picturesque medieval village nestles between two wooded hills, one topped by the huge Norman **Dunster Castle** with its sub-tropical terraced gardens and Jacobean interiors, the other by a folly. It is the perfect spot to stop for a traditional cream tea in one of the quaint tearooms and to browse the pretty shops. At the town's centre is the octagonal Yarn Market, built in 1609 for the sale of the celebrated Dunster cloth. A short stroll south leads to the **Dunster Working Watermill** and picturesque Gallox Bridge, once used by packhorses. On the way look out for the 14th-century Nunnery and St George's Church, which houses an impressive rood screen.

From Dunster, take the
A396 north to the junction
with the A39 and turn left.
At the first roundabout turn
right to **Minehead** seafront. ②

2 MINEHEAD

This handsome seaside resort combines a long sandy beach with an attractive harbour and a charming old town characterised by thatched cottages and narrow alleyways. Walk down the steep Church Steps below St Michael's Church on North Hill to the esplanade and stroll around the harbour, a landing stage for boat trips including the Bristol Channel steam cruisers *Waverley* and *Balmoral*. The seafront marks the start of the long-distance South West Coast Path, which traces the jagged coastline westwards. East along the seafront is the terminus for the **West Somerset Railway**, where you can board a steam train on a nostalgic 40-mile round trip through the scenic Quantock Hills.

Rejoin the A39 travelling
west. After about 2 miles
turn right to **Selworthy**. ③

3 SELWORTHY

Walk through the gate to the National Trust information centre and you'll soon see why this village commands so much attention. Here, hidden from the road by tall hedgerows, cream-coloured thatched cottages with neat gardens cluster photogenically round a village green, overlooked by a pretty church. Built in 1828 for the retired workers of the Holnicote Estate, the village has a delightful homogeny. Above, lies a footpath climbing a mile north to **Selworthy Beacon** from where there are commanding views across the Bristol Channel and Exmoor.

Return to the A39 and turn
right. After about a mile
turn left into **Porlock**. Return
to the A39 and turn left,
then immediately right
onto the B3225 through West
Porlock to **Porlock Weir**.
 ④

From Porlock Weir take the unclassified toll road west to the A39 and turn left. After about half a mile turn right to **Oare** and continue on unclassified roads to **Malmsmead** and **Rockford**.

5

From Rockford continue west on unclassified roads to the B3223. Turn right, then almost immediately right again onto the A39 to **Watersmeet**.

6

Continue on the A39 north west to **Lynmouth**. Take the B3234 out of the town and then the right-hand turn to **Lynton**.

7

Continue from Lynton on the unclassified toll road west into the **Valley of the Rocks** and on to **Woody Bay**.

8

4 PORLOCK AND PORLOCK WEIR

More thatched roofs await in **Porlock**, a quaint village tucked in a hollow between the hills, which invites you to browse the shops and while away the time in tearooms. Porlock is famous for its treacherously steep hill, which leads westwards out of the village; today's cars can negotiate it, but years ago vehicles regularly had to be towed to the top. Instead, head north west to the tiny hamlet of **Porlock Weir,** where a sleepy harbour belies its once vital role as the main route in and out of the area. From here a scenic toll road leads west through the woods to rejoin the main road. At the tollgate there's the start of a one-mile walk west to **Culbone Church**, the smallest parish church in England, set in a peaceful wooded valley.

5 DOONE COUNTRY

The villages of Oare, Malmsmead, Brendon and Rockford lie at the heart of 'Doone Country', the setting for R D Blackmore's famous 1869 novel *Lorna Doone* about a family of outlaws. At **Oare**, you can visit the tiny church where Blackmore's father was rector and where the fictional Lorna was shot at the altar on her wedding day. From here drive west along a scenic road, which hugs the wooded East Lyn Valley towards **Rockford**. Get out of the car en-route at **Malmsmead**, put on your walking boots and take a lovely walk up isolated **Doone Valley** along Badgworthy Water. As you amble through this ancient woodland where silent crooked oaks tower above the tiny stream, it is easy to believe in the colourful stories of the outlaws who lived here and who gave Blackmore inspiration for his novel.

6 WATERSMEET

The thickly wooded beauty spot known as Watersmeet stands at the confluence of two rivers that tumble through a steep gorge in a series of rapids. There are plenty of riverside paths to choose from, or you can simply sit on the veranda of the old fishing lodge (now a National Trust centre) and enjoy a cream tea while watching the water thunder past.

7 LYNMOUTH AND LYNTON

Scenically located at the mouth of the East Lyn River, **Lynmouth** is a traditional fishing village with a cluster of gift shops, a thatched pub and a charming little harbour. The town's tranquil atmosphere was shattered one night in 1952 when torrential rain falling on Exmoor raged down the valley causing much of the village to be washed away. It is hard to imagine such devastation as you wander round the centre today.

Twin town Lynton lies in the upper valley above **Lynmouth** hemmed in by towering cliffs and wooded gorges. The two towns are linked by the ingenious water-powered **Lynton and Lynmouth Cliff Railway**, which affords amazing views. In Lynton, the **Lyn and Exmoor Museum** houses some interesting displays about the area including photos of the flood.

Clockwise from far left:
Valley of the Rocks; Porlock
Bay; harbour, Lynmouth;
horseriders, near Porlock

LITERARY LINKS

Exmoor is best known for its association with
R D Blackmore's novel *Lorna Doone*, but during
the 18th century many writers, including the
poets Wordsworth, Coleridge and Shelley,
sought inspiration from Exmoor's wild and
romantic landscapes. **Lynmouth** is particularly
rich with literary association; it was here that
Coleridge would often walk with Wordsworth,
and where he conceived his *Rime of the Ancient
Mariner*, inspired by Watchet harbour. Shelley
also stayed here with his wife in 1812 in what is
now called **Shelley's Cottage**.

Porlock was a favourite spot of the
Wordsworths, as well as of Robert Southey and
Coleridge, who famously caroused together at
Porlock Weir's Ship Inn. **Ash Farm**, near the tiny
hamlet of Culbone *(below)*, is where Coleridge
is said to have been staying when he wrote his
incomplete poem *Kubla Khan*.

8 VALLEY OF THE ROCKS AND WOODY BAY

West of Lynton the scenery becomes ever more
impressive with jagged rock formations jutting skywards
in the desolate **Valley of the Rocks**, which was described
by Robert Southey as 'the very bones and skeleton of
the earth'. Park the car and climb one of the strange
shattered crags for the stunning sea views – you may
even meet one of the resident wild goats. Back in the
car, the narrow, winding toll road climbs away from the
coast in a series of hairpin bends; it's slow going but
the scenery is spectacular. On a fine day it's worth
stopping at **Woody Bay** where the sheltered rocky
beach is backed by steep wooded cliffs, through which
a fast-flowing stream gushes down to the sea. From
here there is a fabulous two-and-a-half mile cliff walk –
not for the fainthearted – to Heddon's Mouth past one
of the highest waterfalls on this stretch of coast.

*From Woody Bay follow
unclassified roads south to
rejoin the A39, and turn
left heading east. At the
junction with the B3223
turn right to* **Simonsbath**.

 • • • • • • • • • • • • 9

Clockwise from above:
Tarr Steps; Winsford; Dunkery
Beacon, Exmoor National
Park; Withypool

Continue east on the
B3223, then join the
B3224 to Exford. From
Exford take the unclassified
road south west. Cross the
B3223 and continue past
Landacre Bridge to the
junction, then turn
10 *left to Withypool.*

Drive east from Withypool
to join the B3223. Turn right
and after about 2 miles turn
right on the unclassified
11 *road to Tarr Steps.*

Retrace your route to
the B3223. Go straight
across, and continue
on this unclassified
road to Winsford.

→ • • • • • • • • • • **12**

9 SIMONSBATH

The scenery changes dramatically as you climb up from
the coast onto the wild moors and the pretty hamlet of
Simonsbath. It consists of little more than a church, a
handful of cottages and two hotels, but all around the
views stretch endlessly across lonely open moorland
strewn with heather and dotted with distant sheep.
Keep your eyes peeled for the sturdy Exmoor ponies
and wild red deer that roam free near here.

10 EXFORD AND WITHYPOOL

Old cottages cluster round the green in **Exford**, a
popular centre for riders and walkers, situated on an
ancient crossing point on the River Exe. Enjoy a
refreshing drink at one of the quaint old inns before
setting off to neighbouring **Withypool**, a tiny unspoilt
village set around an old stone bridge. On the way, take
a slight detour west to stop off at **Landacre Bridge**, a
local beauty spot, ideal on a hot day for a picnic by the
river and dipping your toes in the clear, icy water.

11 TARR STEPS

This ancient clapper bridge, believed to date from the
Middle Ages, is the finest of its type in Britain, with
huge stone slabs set across 17 spans. The stones look as
though they have been here forever, but in fact they
have been frequently replaced throughout their history.
In the famous Lynmouth floods of 1952 all but one were
washed away. Most days, it is a tranquil little spot,
perfect for an afternoon snooze. The stunning
moorland scenery all around makes this whole area
hugely popular with horseriders. If you fancy a short
trek, there are several stables in the vicinity offering
rides for all levels of ability.

EXMOOR ON FOOT

The landscape of Exmoor is tremendously
varied, from rolling farmland and high, wild
moorland to a dramatic and tantalisingly
beautiful coastline. Britain's longest national
trail, the **South West Coast Path** *(below)*,
follows the coast west from Minehead along
lofty cliffs interspersed with isolated rocky
coves, carved by wind and waves. It offers some
of the most rewarding, and often challenging,
coastal walking in Britain. Exmoor's other
famous long-distance route, the **Two Moors
Way**, begins at Lynmouth on its 102-mile
journey south to Ivybridge on the southern
edge of Dartmoor, crossing the high moors of
Exmoor's remote and tranquil interior before
dipping into its deep wooded fringes. There are
also a plethora of shorter footpaths as well as
a regular schedule of guided walks with park
rangers. For more information contact the
Exmoor National Park Authority.

12 WINSFORD

A scattering of thatched cottages around an attractive green and no fewer than eight bridges and a ford make this one of the most photographed villages on the moor. On the way here from Tarr Steps you will pass a footpath off to the right, leading to the **Caratacus Stone**, an ancient monolith bearing an inscription to Caratacus, the last great Celtic chieftain.

13 DUNKERY BEACON

It is a relatively easy half-mile walk from the car park up to the stone beacon that marks Exmoor's highest point at 519m (1700ft). On a clear day you can drink in views stretching across 16 counties from the Brecon Beacons in the north to Dartmoor in the south. You should also be able to make out the little church at Selworthy, a white silhouette clearly visible against the green bulk of Selworthy Hill.

Take the unclassified road north east to the A396 and turn left to Wheddon Cross. Turn left in the village onto the B3224. At the bend take the second right turn and follow the unclassified road to *Dunkery Beacon* car park. ⑬

Continue north on unclassified roads to Luccombe, then head east via Wootton Courtenay to return to **Dunster**.

WITH MORE TIME

South of Exmoor, two of the region's finest historic gems beckon. **Knightshayes Court** *(left)* is a Victorian Gothic mansion designed by flamboyant architect William Burges, with elegant formal terraces and topiary. To the east lies the beautiful medieval house of **Cothay Manor and Gardens**, which is set in romantic gardens. Further east near Taunton is another worthwhile visit, **Hestercombe Gardens**, where the fabulous grounds have been painstakingly restored and include a secret landscape garden complete with lake and temples.

Inland from the Jurassic Coast

Walk along the dramatic beaches of the West Dorset coast and 185 million years of history unfold before your eyes. This is part of the breathtakingly beautiful, 95-mile long Jurassic Coast, which was awarded World Heritage status in 2001. Once an area of swamp and lagoons where dinosaurs roamed at the end of the Jurassic period, it is now a rich hunting ground for fossils. Inland, hidden among the rolling hills, are lush gardens, gorgeous stone cottages and little-known treasure houses, as well as the opportunity to sample some of England's finest home-grown produce.

TOUR ROUTE

Lyme Regis ①
Golden Cap ②
Bridport ③
Crewkerne ④
East Lambrook Manor Gardens
  and Kingsbury Episcopi ⑤
Barrington Court ⑥
Forde Abbey ⑦
Colyton and the Seaton Tramway ⑧
Branscombe ⑨
Beer ⑩

TOUR LENGTH

DISTANCE approx. 78 miles (126km)

DURATION 2 days

TOURIST INFORMATION CENTRES

BRIDPORT 47 South St, DT6 3NY;
01308 424901

LYME REGIS Guildhall Cottage, Church St,
DT7 3BS; 01297 442138

SEATON The Underfleet, EX12 2TB;
01297 21660

Miles 0 _____ 5
Kms 0 _____ 5

1 LYME REGIS

Narrow streets lined with shops, cafes and fine Georgian houses rise steeply from the sea in this lovely resort, best known as the setting for the film *The French Lieutenant's Woman* (based on John Fowles' novel). The handsome harbour, which huddles in the shelter of its curved stone breakwater, known as **The Cobb**, is where the cloaked heroine of the film famously stood gazing out to sea. The breakwater is also a key setting in Jane Austen's novel *Persuasion*.

   Lyme Regis is world famous for its bountiful fossils, which emerge with astonishing frequency from the crumbling cliffs. The most famous find was in 1811 when 12-year-old Mary Anning uncovered a complete 6m (21ft) icthyosaurus skeleton, now on display in London's Natural History Museum. You can find out more at the excellent **Philpot Museum**, which houses many finds. Or if you fancy fossil hunting yourself, one of the best areas is the beach between Lyme Regis and neighbouring **Charmouth**; but beware of the tide and crumbling cliffs. The Philpot Museum together with the **Charmouth Heritage Coast Centre** and **Dinosaurland** (two other magnets for avid fossil collectors) give advice and run regular guided fossil collecting walks. Alternatively, you can always treat yourself to an ammonite from one of the many shops selling fossils.

2 GOLDEN CAP

At a height of 190m (625ft), Golden Cap is the highest sea cliff along the south coast – the far-reaching views from the summit simply take the breath away. As you climb the steep path west from the little hamlet of Seatown, close your eyes for a moment and inhale the heavy, sweet scent of gorse mingled with the invigorating sea air. For an enjoyable round trip, continue west to the abandoned hamlet of **Stanton St Gabriel**: its now-ruined chapel was reputedly used by smugglers to hide casks of brandy. Then return to Seatown for a well-earned drink at the village inn.

Clockwise from far left:
Jurassic Coast, near the Golden Cap; The Cobb, Lyme Regis; harbour, Lyme Regis; church, Branscombe; view from the Golden Cap

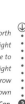
From Lyme Regis head north on the A3052 and turn right onto the A35. Continue to Chideock, then turn right onto the steep, narrow unclassified road to Seatown and Golden Cap. **2**

Return to the A35 and turn right in to Bridport.
 3

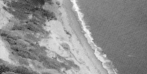

Clockwise from above:
Forde Abbey; gardens,
Barrington Court

⊕ Take the B3162 north to the
B3165 and turn right to
④ **Crewkerne**.

⊕ Drive north on the A356
out of Crewkerne for about
one mile then turn left on
unclassified roads via South
Petherton to *East Lambrook
Manor Gardens* and then
⑤ on to *Kingsbury Episcopi*.

*From Kingsbury
Episcopi drive south west
on unclassified roads
through Stembridge to
Barrington Court.*

→ • • • • • • • • • • ⑥

HOME GROWN

There is nothing that quite beats the taste of
fresh home produce, and this part of England
offers plenty of opportunities to buy some of
the country's finest. **Brown and Forrest** *(below)*,
a traditional family-run smokery in Langport,
produces excellent smoked eel and salmon, as
well as smoked chicken, duck, lamb and trout.
For a real taste of Somerset cider visit **Perry's
Cider** in the picturesque village of Dowlish
Wake near Ilminster, where you can sample
award-winning speciality ciders produced in
the 16th-century thatched barn. And if you
fancy picking your own fruit stop
off at **Forde Abbey Fruit Farm**.

3 BRIDPORT
_____

A vibrant and colourful town set amongst the West
Dorset hills, Bridport is dominated by a Georgian town
hall and broad, wide open streets offering views of the
countryside beyond. The town's long history as the
centre of the country's rope- and net-making industry
is explored in the **Bridport Museum**.

4 CREWKERNE
_____

The attractive market town of Crewkerne features
many fine buildings, art, antique and book shops and a
striking 15th-century church made from the locally
quarried, honey-coloured hamstone. The town's history
is recounted at the **Crewkerne Heritage Centre** with
displays on the Saxon mint, the famous grammar
school and the town's cloth-making past.

5 EAST LAMBROOK MANOR GARDENS
AND KINGSBURY EPISCOPI
_____

East Lambrook Manor Gardens is the quintessential
English cottage garden, boasting colourful herbaceous
borders, overspilling with flowers, set against the
backdrop of a golden stone house. The garden was
created by the late Margery Fish and houses a nursery
selling many rare and unusual plants.

Just to the north lies the traditional hamstone village
of **Kingsbury Episcopi**, where there's a lovely church and
an ancient lock-up cell on the green. The village is set in the
heart of cider country and you can visit **Somerset Cider
Brandy**, one of the region's oldest producers, to see the
old oak vats and copper stills, walk round the orchards
and sample some of the delicious finished product.

6 BARRINGTON COURT

Garden lovers will want to linger in the beautiful and elegant gardens at Barrington Court, which are laid out as a series of themed 'rooms', including the enchanting lily garden and the white garden with its cool and carefully coordinated silvers and creams. The Tudor manor house now houses an antique furniture showroom.

7 FORDE ABBEY

Reached by winding country lanes, Forde Abbey is one of rural England's best-kept secrets. The house, dating from 1140, was once a Cistercian monastery and contains some magnificent tapestries depicting cartoons by Raphael. The gardens are equally impressive, set in 12ha (30 acres) and including five lakes, a bog garden and a wonderful working kitchen garden where serried rows of vegetables stand to attention.

8 COLYTON AND THE SEATON TRAMWAY

Tucked away at the head of the River Axe, the little Saxon town of **Colyton** lies at the start of the scenic narrow-gauge tram ride to the coast at Seaton. The three-mile **Seaton Tramway** runs alongside the verdant Axe Estuary, teeming with wading birds and other wildlife. As you set off look out for Colyton's landmark St Andrew's Church; its tower was once used to guide ships up the estuary. Seaton itself boasts a fine promenade, harbour and some lovely parks and gardens where you can stretch your legs before your return journey. On the way back, you could stop off at pretty **Colyford**, where there's an old petrol station housing a motor museum.

9 BRANSCOMBE

This idyllic coastal village, featuring pretty rows of rose-bedecked cottages, a church and fine pubs, is believed to be the longest village in Britain. A cluster of National Trust-owned buildings here include the old thatched **Forge** where blacksmiths can be seen at work, the restored water-powered **Manor Mill**, and the thatched **Old Bakery**, where you can enjoy a heavenly cream tea, by a roaring open fire in winter.

10 BEER

One of the scenic jewels of this stretch of coastline, the attractive little port of Beer nestles in a sheltered cove between tall chalk cliffs, with a tiny stream flowing through its centre. The village is renowned for its history of lacemaking, and you'll still find some lace for sale in the gift shops that line the main street. In 1839, 100 Beer lacemakers produced the trimmings for Queen Victoria's wedding dress for the princely cost of £1,000.

Wander down to the beach with its painted bathing huts and brightly coloured boats on the shingle, and then visit **Beer Quarry Caves**, where for 2,000 years chalk limestone has been hewn by hand – some of it used in notable buildings around the country including Westminster Abbey. The labyrinth of caverns hide a secret Catholic chapel used during times of religious persecution; the caves were also a favourite hiding spot for smugglers in the 18th and early 19th centuries, including the notorious Jack Rattenbury.

Continue south on unclassified roads across the A303 through Ilminster and Dowlish Wake to the A30. Turn right on the A30, then almost immediately left onto the B3167. After about one mile, turn left onto the B3162, then right onto the unclassified road to **Forde Abbey**. **7**

Travel west on unclassified roads to the B3167 and turn left to join the A358, heading south through Axminster to the junction with the A3052. Turn right then right again on the B3161 to **Colyton** *and the* **Seaton Tramway**. **8**

Return to the A3052 and turn right. After about 3 miles turn left on the unclassified road south to **Branscombe**. **9**

Continue on unclassified roads heading east to **Beer**. **10**

Take the B3172 east to the junction with the A3052, then turn right to return to **Lyme Regis**. **1**

WITH MORE TIME

Just along the coast from Beer is the genteel resort of **Sidmouth** *(left)*, characterised by elegant Regency architecture, beautiful gardens and a wide esplanade. The resort's picturesque setting between majestic red cliffs at the mouth of the River Sid and its inviting sand and pebble beach made it fashionable with the upper classes in the 19th century, many of whom built grand residences here. Just west of town is the popular Jacob's Ladder beach, while to the east, on Salcombe Hill is the Norman Lockyer Observatory, with its large telescopes and planetarium.

Thomas Hardy's Dorset

Associations with the novelist and poet Thomas Hardy are to be found at almost every twist and turn in his homeland of Wessex. The rolling hills, hedgerow-bordered lanes, quaint villages and historic market towns steeped in tales of intrigue all provide the backdrop against which Hardy's characters act out their fate. Serene country houses set in gorgeous gardens invite exploration, as does the dramatic World Heritage Coast, which reveals a succession of extraordinary rock formations created by the pounding of waves over millions of years.

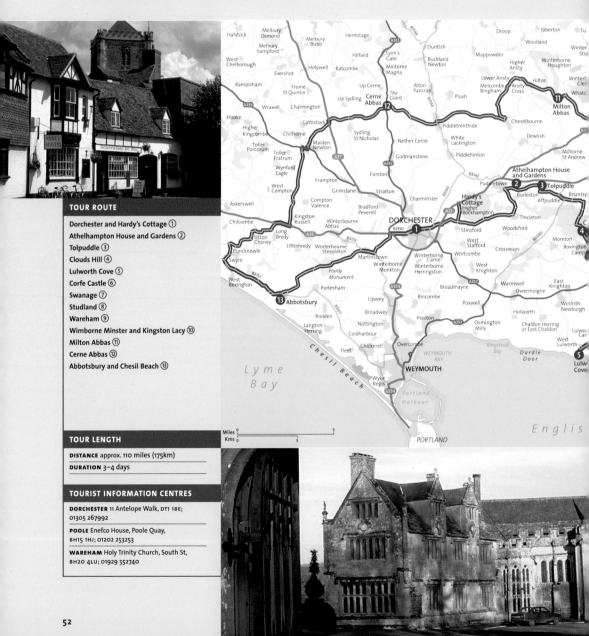

TOUR ROUTE

Dorchester and Hardy's Cottage ①
Athelhampton House and Gardens ②
Tolpuddle ③
Clouds Hill ④
Lulworth Cove ⑤
Corfe Castle ⑥
Swanage ⑦
Studland ⑧
Wareham ⑨
Wimborne Minster and Kingston Lacy ⑩
Milton Abbas ⑪
Cerne Abbas ⑫
Abbotsbury and Chesil Beach ⑬

TOUR LENGTH

DISTANCE approx. 110 miles (175km)
DURATION 3–4 days

TOURIST INFORMATION CENTRES

DORCHESTER 11 Antelope Walk, DT1 1BE;
01305 267992

POOLE Enefco House, Poole Quay,
BH15 1HJ; 01202 253253

WAREHAM Holy Trinity Church, South St,
BH20 4LU; 01929 552740

1 DORCHESTER AND HARDY'S COTTAGE

If Thomas Hardy's spirit roams anywhere, it is around this attractive old market town – the fictional Casterbridge of his famous novel *The Mayor of Casterbridge*. This is where he went to school, trained as an architect and lived for 40 years in the house he designed at **Max Gate**. Hardy's impressive legacy is highlighted in the **Dorset County Museum**, which has the largest collection of Hardy memorabilia in the world, and commemorated by a statue on High Street West, which portrays the writer as an elderly man. Just three miles north east of Dorchester, **Hardy's Cottage** at Higher Bockhampton is particularly popular with literary pilgrims. The pretty thatched cottage is where the writer was born and wrote many of his finest works.

Judge Jeffrey's Restaurant on High Street West is a reminder of Dorchester's chequered past. This is the former home of the infamous 'hanging judge', sent here to punish the supporters of the Duke of Monmouth's unsuccessful rebellion in 1685. A series of trials known as the Bloody Assizes saw 74 rebels hung, drawn and quartered and 175 transported to the West Indian colonies for slave labour. Almost as notorious was the fate of the Tolpuddle Martyrs *(see p54)* who were held in cells at the **Old Crown Court**, which can be visited by guided tour in summer. Behind the High Street you can visit the impressive **Roman Town House**, an excavated Roman villa with a preserved mosaic floor. Dorchester also boasts its own Roman amphitheatre, the **Maumbury Rings** on the southern edge of town, which is still used today for outdoor performances.

2 ATHELHAMPTON HOUSE AND GARDENS

The rooms inside this fine 15th-century house are magnificently furnished and brimming with architectural interest, particularly the Tudor Great Hall featuring a timbered roof, minstrels' gallery and richly detailed heraldic glass, and the oak-panelled Great Chamber with its secret passageway. Surrounding the house are 8ha (20 acres) of gardens with a series of lovely vistas; the Great Court contains 12 giant yew pyramids and eight walled gardens.

Clockwise from far left: Dorchester; Hardy's Cottage; statue, Abbotsbury Sub-Tropical Gardens; Athelhampton House and Gardens

*Take the B3150 east out of Dorchester. At the junction with the A35 cross over onto the unclassified road to Stinsford and continue east. For **Hardy's Cottage**, detour left at the first crossroads after Stinsford. For **Athelhampton House and Gardens** turn left at Tincleton and then right.* **2**

*Continue east on unclassified roads through Burleston to **Tolpuddle**.*

 3

⊕ *Drive east on unclassified*
• *roads through Affpuddle to*
• *Briantspuddle. Turn right in*
• *the village and continue*
• *south for about 2 miles*
❹ *to Clouds Hill.*

3 TOLPUDDLE

The little village of Tolpuddle was put on the world map by six farm labourers who – in response to their intolerable living conditions – established a trade union here in 1883. Their actions led to their arrest and ultimately the foundation of modern-day trade unionism: their story is told at the **Tolpuddle Martyrs Museum**. Only one of the martyrs was ever to return here; the others, following their pardon, emigrated to Canada.

4 CLOUDS HILL

You can almost picture T E Lawrence in this tiny cottage, as the rooms remain just as he left them, filled with his simple furnishings and wartime photographs, the walls lined with books. The well-known soldier and author, better known as Lawrence of Arabia, rented Clouds Hill in 1923 as a retreat from army life while serving at nearby Bovington Camp. Tragically, he was killed in a motorbike accident on his way home here just five days after being discharged from the army.

⊕ *Continue south on*
• *unclassified roads through*
• *Bovington Camp, and then*
• *right onto the A352. Turn*
• *left almost immediately*
• *onto the B3071/B3070*
• *to West Lulworth and*
❺ *Lulworth Cove.*

5 LULWORTH COVE

It is not just geologists who marvel over the graceful line of this natural horseshoe-shaped bay, which was formed some 10,000 years ago. Lulworth Cove sits at the western end of the Isle of Purbeck, where the spectacular coastline has been awarded World Heritage status. Bring a picnic and some walking boots and follow the coastal path one mile west to view the striking limestone archway of **Durdle Door**. Or for even better views, catch the motorboat launch, which sails in the summer from Lulworth beach to Mupe Bay and Durdle Door. You can find out more about the history and geology of the area at **Lulworth's Heritage Centre** in West Lulworth.

Drive north east on the
B3070, turn right just
before East Lulworth and
follow unclassified roads to
Corfe Castle.

↪ • • • • • • • • • • ❻

THE HARDY TRAIL

Thomas Hardy's novels and poems are rich in depictions of rural life and the struggles of country folk set against the backdrop of his native land. A well-established trail explores the gentle Dorset countryside so beloved by the writer *(below)*, taking in many of the towns and villages that feature in his works. Among those identifiable are Dorchester (Casterbridge in *The Mayor of Casterbridge*), Bournemouth (Sandbourne in *Tess of the D'Urbervilles*), Bere Regis (Kingsbere in *Tess of the D'Urbervilles*) and Stinsford (Mellstock in *Under the Greenwood Tree*). Other Hardy landmarks forming part of the trail include Sturminster Newton where Hardy and his wife Emma had their first real home together, Stinsford's churchyard where Hardy's heart is buried in his wife's grave and Hardy's birthplace at Higher Bockhampton. A free leaflet outlining the trail is available from tourist information centres in the area.

6 CORFE CASTLE

Sweeping sea views will accompany your drive east from the coast up onto the chalk ridge of the Purbeck Hills, before dropping down to Corfe. The village is dominated by the majestic ruins of its castle, which once guarded a strategic gap in the hills. The history of the castle is a long and bloody one: the young King Edward was murdered by his stepmother here in AD978 and, in the 12th century, 22 knights were starved to death in the dungeons on the order of King John. Although blown up during the Civil War, the ruins still retain many fine features, in particular the Horseshoe Tower, which survives almost to its original height.

7 SWANAGE

Up until the 19th century, Swanage was the main centre for the transportation of Purbeck marble, used to decorate churches and cathedrals around the country. Today, it is a seaside town with a sandy beach and restored Victorian pier, and the terminus for the scenic **Swanage Railway** with steam trains huffing and puffing their way six miles inland past Corfe Castle. A leisurely stroll from the seafront towards the town centre brings you to the picturesque Mill Pond in the oldest and most attractive part of town.

On the clifftops above Swanage lies **Durlston Country Park**, 113 ha (280 acres) of land perfect for walking, picnicking or just taking in the fantastic views of the Isle of Wight across Swanage Bay. Its main man-made feature is the massive Great Globe, made from Portland limestone and carved with a world map. It was placed here in 1887 by John Mowlem, one of Swanage's most successful stone and building contractors.

Clockwise from far left:
Durdle Door, near Lulworth Cove; Great Globe, Durlston Country Park; castle ruins, Corfe Castle

8 STUDLAND

Much of this pretty village, which is clustered around a Norman church, lies in the hands of the National Trust. It is an ideal spot to take a break from driving and relax on its white, sandy, shell-strewn beach, which stretches for three miles from Shell Bay to the crumbling chalk stacks of Old Harry Rocks. Behind the beach, nature trails – rich in birdlife – lead through the sand dunes. For a particularly rewarding walk, climb to the Agglestone, a 5m-high boulder (16ft), which according to legend was hurled here by the Devil as he sat on the Needles on the Isle of Wight; his intended target was Salisbury Cathedral! The South West Coast Path also begins its 630-mile journey west from **Studland Bay** to Minehead *(see p43)* in north Somerset, offering stunning coastal walks.

Take the A351 south east to Swanage. **7**

*Drive north out of Swanage on the unclassified road and then turn right on the B3351 to **Studland**.* **8**

*Head west on the B3351 to Corfe Castle then turn right onto the A351 and join the B3075 right to **Wareham**.*  **9**

⊕ *Continue north on the A351*
and then take the B3075
left to Winterbourne
Zelston. Turn right onto the
*A31 to **Wimborne Minster**.*
From Wimborne Minster
take the B3082 north west
⑩ *to **Kingston Lacy**.*

9 WAREHAM

Wareham's old quay gives a clue to this inland town's former role as Dorset's principal port, and is a good place to begin a stroll round this charming town. Wareham has played an important part in Dorset's history: it was here that the boy King Edward was buried without ceremony after his murder at Corfe Castle, while the now-named Bloody Bank along the town walls was the spot chosen by Judge Jeffreys to hang some of the Monmouth rebels.

On the northern edge of town, the preserved Saxon **St Martin's Church** houses medieval wall paintings and a marble effigy of T E Lawrence *(see p54)*. Just south of Wareham (off the A351) is the **Blue Pool**, an idyllic beauty spot where the water changes colour according to variations in the weather, a phenomenon caused by the reflective properties of the clay in the water.

10 WIMBORNE MINSTER AND KINGSTON LACY

The delightful market town of Wimborne Minster is dominated by the twin spires of its medieval **minster**, which boasts a magnificent Norman nave and arches. Of particular interest is the Chained Library above the choir vestry, founded in 1686 as a free library for the townspeople. Look out for the Quarter Jack on the west tower – a brightly painted figure of a grenadier, which still strikes the quarter hours.

Just west of town lies the 17th-century estate of **Kingston Lacy**. This elegant country mansion owes its outstanding art collection to W J Bankes, a friend of Lord Byron. Shortly after inheriting the house, Bankes became involved in a sexual scandal and fled to Italy, from where he continued to send shipments of artefacts right up to his death. The treasures survive today and include paintings by Rubens, Titian and Van Dyck as well as ornate ceilings, Egyptian antiquities and a magnificent marble staircase. The house is set in attractive formal gardens and surrounded by 100ha (250 acres) of wooded parkland, with lovely waymarked walks and magnificent snowdrop displays in early spring.

*Continue north west on the B3082, turn left on unclassified roads through Sturminster Marshall and cross the A350 to the A31. Turn right on the A31, and after about 3 miles turn right again following unclassified roads through Winterborne Kingston and Whitechurch. Cross the A354 and continue north west to **Milton Abbas**.*

→ • • • • • • • • • • • ⑪

Clockwise from right:
Tithe Barn, Abbotsbury; ceiling, Wimborne Minster; St Catherine's Chapel, Abbotsbury; Giant, Cerne Abbas; Kingston Lacy

Follow unclassified roads to Ansty Cross and then south to Cheselbourne and west via Piddletrenthide to **Cerne Abbas.** **12**

11 MILTON ABBAS

Only the 15th-century **abbey** remains of the old town of Middleton, demolished in the 1770s by Lord Milton and rebuilt nearby as Milton Abbas in a place where it would not mar the view from his house. The 'new' village is an enchanting place to visit with its identical thatched cottages lining the main street.

12 CERNE ABBAS

Most people visit Cerne Abbas to see the **Giant**, a huge, naked, club-wielding figure cut into the chalk hillside above the town. His association with springtime fertility rites has led to the theory that he is a representation of the Roman hero-god Hercules, though no one knows for certain. In Victorian times, the grass was encouraged to grow over what were considered to be his offensive parts, but they have since been allowed to reappear. Little remains of the abbey that gave the village its name, but it's certainly worth wandering round the streets, which are full of old world charm. Look out for the **Pitchmarket**, opposite the church on Abbey Street, one in a row of fine Tudor houses and the purported home of Thomas Washington (uncle of the American president) in the 18th century.

13 ABBOTSBURY AND CHESIL BEACH

As you approach Abbotsbury from the west, the view of the village – nestling around its church in a patchwork of green with the great shingle ridge of Chesil Beach stretching endlessly beyond – is simply stunning. This is a gem of a village with picturesque thatched cottages and welcoming pubs and tearooms. The 11th-century Benedictine abbey is long gone, but the abbey gateway and **Abbotsbury Tithe Barn** still make an impressive sight, as does **St Catherine's Chapel**, which guards the village from its perch on a lonely hill. Down on the Fleet Lagoon is the famous **Abbotsbury Swannery**, where a huge colony of mute swans have been breeding in sheltered waters for over 600 years. Leave some time to visit the **Abbotsbury Sub-Tropical Gardens**, just outside the village, where palm trees flourish and camellias and magnolias create a blaze of colour in spring.

Continue on foot south east from Abbotsbury to Chesil Beach and explore this remarkable shingle spit, 12m-high (40ft) in places and stretching for 10 miles to the Isle of Portland. One of its most curious features is the gradual degradation in the size of the pebbles from east to west, which is so precise that local fishermen landing on the beach at night can tell where they are by the size of the stones.

Drive west on unclassified roads to Maiden Newton, turn right onto the A356 then almost immediately left, continuing south on unclassified roads to Kingston Russell. Turn briefly right onto the A35, then left following unclassified roads south west to Swyre. Turn left onto the B3157 to **Abbotsbury** *and* **Chesil Beach.** **13**

Take the narrow unclassified road from Abbotsbury north east to the B3159. Turn right through Martinstown then shortly after turn left and continue to the A35 to return and follow the B3150 to return to **Dorchester.**

← • • • • • • • • • • • ❶

WITH MORE TIME

Sheltered by one of the largest natural harbours in the world, **Poole** is a busy port with an attractive quay lined with old houses, restaurants and pubs as well as the Poole Pottery Factory Outlet. From the quay, a regular ferry service sails to Brownsea Island *(left)*. Set at the entrance to Poole harbour, with spectacular views of the Purbeck Hills, this lovely wooded island is one of the few places where red squirrels still thrive, and it is an idyllic place to walk or picnic. The northern part of the island is a nature reserve, home to red deer and more than 200 bird species.

57

On the trail of King Arthur

The rolling hills of Somerset and Dorset are blanketed with a patchwork of pretty stone villages, stately homes and lovingly tended gardens, and their wonderful, sleepy back roads make them ideal for cycling and leisurely driving. Scattered with historic castles, glorious cathedrals and mysterious caves, the area is loaded with headline attractions. However, it is also awash with sacred sites, prehistoric hill forts and mystical ley lines, all of which gave rise to rich local lore offering strong links with the legend of King Arthur and his band of knights. Whether these tales have any historic truth or not, the area brims with intrigue.

TOUR ROUTE

Sherborne ①
Montacute House ②
Somerton ③
Street ④
Glastonbury ⑤
Cheddar Caves and Gorge ⑥
Wookey Hole Caves ⑦
Wells ⑧
Shepton Mallet ⑨
Mells ⑩
Nunney Castle ⑪
Bruton ⑫
Cadbury Castle ⑬
Fleet Air Arm Museum ⑭

TOUR LENGTH

DISTANCE approx. 90 miles (145km)

DURATION 3 days

TOURIST INFORMATION CENTRES

GLASTONBURY The Tribunal, 9 High St, BA6 9DP; 01458 832954

SHERBORNE 3 Tilton Court, Digby Rd, DT9 3NL; 01935 815341

WELLS Town Hall, Market Pl, BA5 2RB; 01749 672552

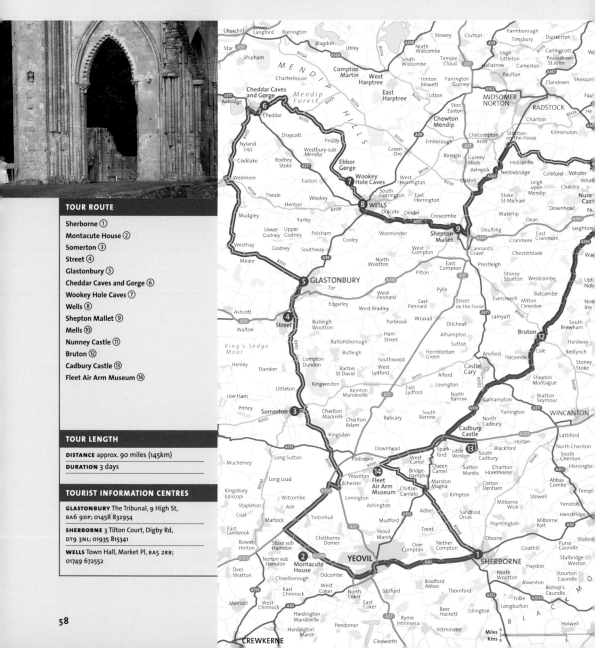

1 SHERBORNE

Once the capital of Wessex, the pretty town of Sherborne, with its winding streets and red stone buildings, is a sleepy but charming place. Sherborne was a cathedral city until Old Sarum *(see p65)* took the honour in 1075, and its wonderful church, **Sherborne Abbey**, was built on the remains of the 8th-century cathedral. The church is a fine example of 15th-century Perpendicular style, and its most impressive features are the delicate fan vaulting – the oldest in the country – and a set of beautiful misericords on the choir stalls. The medieval **Almshouse** in the abbey close is one of only a few in the country that still fulfils its original role. Nearby on Church Lane, you'll find the **Sherborne Museum**, which chronicles the history of the town's fortunes.

Also worth visiting is **Sherborne House**, a Palladian mansion built in 1720, which is currently under restoration. The house is now used for local art exhibitions but its most glorious asset is the baroque mural of the Calydonian hunt and Goddess Diana in the hall, painted by Dorset artist Sir James Thornhill.

Sherborne is most famous for its two castles. **Sherborne Old Castle**, 'a malicious and malevolent' place according to Cromwell, was a much-coveted 12th-century fortress. Queen Elizabeth I granted it to Sir Walter Raleigh in the late 16th century, and although he spent a fortune on alterations, it never lived up to his lofty expectations and he soon moved across the river and began work on the new **Sherborne Castle**. When Raleigh fell out of favour with the court in 1617, the castle was sold to the Digby family who have been there ever since. Expect fine Gothic interiors brimming with artworks, period furniture and porcelain and – from the landscaped grounds – a view of the ruined old castle destroyed by Cromwellian troops in 1645.

Clockwise from far left:
Glastonbury Abbey;
Glastonbury Tor; Sherborne
Abbey; window, Wells
Cathedral; Wookey Hole Caves

*Take the A30 west from Sherborne and turn right onto the A3088 south of Yeovil, then follow the signs left to **Montacute House**.*

KING ARTHUR & THE ISLE OF AVALON

God-like king, parable of virtue or mythical hero, King Arthur and the tales of his legendary escapades have endured through the centuries and yet no one is sure whether he actually existed. Just as contentious is Glastonbury's claim to be the mythical Isle of Avalon where Excalibur (King Arthur's sword) was forged, where his sister Morgan le Fay lived and where Arthur was brought to die. It was only in the 12th century that Glastonbury came to be associated with Avalon. A great fire devastated the monastery, and just seven years later a band of resourceful monks 'found' Arthur's grave in the grounds. The streams of pilgrims that followed brought significant wealth to the abbey for its reconstruction. Additional local stories about Joseph of Arimathea, the Holy Grail, the healing well waters and the causeway to Cadbury Castle *(see p63)*, thought to be legendary Camelot, all support Glastonbury's claim to be the Isle of Avalon. Whether it is elaborate early spin or historical truth no one really knows; either way the town and its sacred sites continue to hold a mystical and powerful pull that is difficult to ignore.

↓ *Continue north west on the A3088, then turn right onto the A303 in to central Ilchester and take the B3151*
3 *north to Somerton.*

2 MONTACUTE HOUSE

One of England's finest Elizabethan mansions, Montacute House was built in 1590 for Sir Edward Phelips, a lawyer and politician known for giving the prosecution's opening speech at the trial of Guy Fawkes. The stunning house with its carved parapets and elegant chimneys has equally impressive interiors with elaborate plasterwork, opulent textiles and period furniture, which made it an ideal location for the filming of *Sense and Sensibility*. The grand state rooms play host to a fine collection of Tudor and Elizabethan portraits on permanent loan from the National Portrait Gallery, and outside the impressive landscaped grounds include formal gardens.

↓ *Continue north on the B3151*
4 *to Street.*

3 SOMERTON

Somerton was the capital of Wessex in the 7th century until Alfred the Great established Winchester as the new seat of government. Today it is a lovely, mellow town with a wide 17th-century square, an octagonal market cross, a town hall and some elegant houses and inns. The parish **church** contains one of the finest wooden roofs in the county, carved by the monks of nearby Muchelney Abbey. In summer, a programme of events includes the popular week-long Somerton Arts Festival, which takes place every July.

4 STREET

Local farmer and devout Quaker Cyrus Clark set up a sheepskin and shoe-making business in Street in 1825, and the town became internationally known as the home base of C & J Clark Ltd, whose headquarters still border the High Street. Street now boasts a major factory outlet shopping complex – **Clarks Village** – attracting visitors from far and wide with more than 75 individual shop units, many of which are household-name companies, selling quality goods at discount prices.

Drive further north on the B3151 to Glastonbury.

→ • • • • • • • • • • • **5**

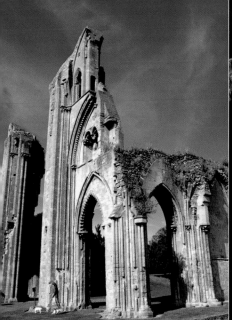

Clockwise from far left:
gardens, Montacute House;
Glastonbury Abbey;
Wookey Hole Caves;
market cross, Somerton

5 GLASTONBURY

Although more famous today for its music festival than its mystical connections, bohemian Glastonbury lies at the heart of numerous ancient legends and at the crossing point of powerful ley lines. The town has attracted those in search of spiritual enlightenment for centuries, and today it is bursting with wholefood, incense and healers.

The once majestic **Glastonbury Abbey** was allegedly founded by Joseph of Arimathea, a kinsman of Christ who owned mines in the nearby Mendip Hills. According to local legend he arrived here with the Holy Grail (the chalice used in the Last Supper), planted his staff in the earth, saw it sprout a thorn bush and began his quest to bring Christianity to England. Officially however, the abbey evolved out of a Celtic monastery, founded in the 4th or 5th century, and grew into a wealthy Benedictine abbey after the bodies of King Arthur and Queen Guinevere were allegedly found in the grounds. The abbey, however, was decimated during the Protestant Reformation and all that remains today are the evocative ruins. Joseph's Holy Grail was supposedly hidden in the nearby **Chalice Well**, an iron-red spring surrounded by tranquil gardens. The water from the well is unlikely to have been coloured by the blood of Christ as local legend suggests, but many believe it does have curative powers.

Just east of town, rising spectacularly above the plains is **Glastonbury Tor**, a conical hill topped by St Michael's Tower and the ruins of a 14th-century church. It is a truly mystical place with incredible views over the surrounding countryside that gives a real sense of why this town and area has inspired writers, poets and healers for centuries.

6 CHEDDAR CAVES AND GORGE

Known for its eponymous cheese, Cheddar pulls in the crowds who come to explore its dramatic gorge and limestone caves. The caves were formed during the last Ice Age creating amazing rock formations in **Gough's Cave**. A 40,000-year-old skeleton discovered in **Cox's Cave** has helped prove the theory that they were used as shelter for primitive families. Just outside the cave the steep steps of Jacob's Ladder lead to vantage points with stunning views of Exmoor, Glastonbury Tor and the sea. From here you can walk along the top of the spectacular steep-sided gorge – it is a far more peaceful route than the drive through the gorge on the narrow winding road below.

7 WOOKEY HOLE CAVES

The impressive series of caves at Wookey Hole were carved by the River Axe over millions of years. They feature some magnificent underground chambers with incredible stalactites and stalagmites, as well as an eerie subterranean lake where dramatic light and sound effects bring the caves' natural wonder to life. Here too, supposedly, is the final resting place of the Witch of Wookey Hole, a woman reputed to have cast her evil eye on locals. Legend has it, she was finally stopped in her tracks and turned to stone when a monk sprinkled her with holy water.

Travel north west on the B3151 to Cheddar, then turn right onto the A371 and left onto the B3135 to **Cheddar Caves and Gorge**. **6**

Drive through the gorge on the B3135 and turn right on unclassified roads through the village of Priddy to Ebbor Gorge and **Wookey Hole Caves**. **7**

From Wookey Hole, drive south east on unclassified roads to **Wells**.
 **8**

Clockwise from above:
nave, Wells Cathedral;
Nunney Castle; Fleet
Air Arm Museum; façade,
Wells Cathedral

*Drive east on the
A371 to **Shepton**
9 **Mallet**.*

8 WELLS

Charming, understated Wells hides its treasures from
prying eyes, and it is only when you walk from the
Market Square into the Cathedral Close that you spy
the magnificent Early English Gothic **cathedral** for the
first time. Set back on the green lawns and presiding
over the surrounding medieval buildings in the close, the
cathedral reveals a fanfare of 300 figures on the recently
restored west front. Inside, giant scissor arches take the
weight of the central tower and wonderful capitals and
corbels line the nave. Look out for the astronomical
clock dating from 1392, and then climb the stone steps
to the stunning Chapter House.

Before leaving the close stroll around to the **Vicar's Close,**
a gorgeous lane said to be the oldest continually inhabited street in Europe. Next to the cathedral on Market
Square is the imposing **Bishop's Palace**, a 13th-century
monument with Gothic state rooms, a moat fed by the
springs that give the town its name and its own bevy of
swans trained to ring a bell whenever they need feeding.

*Head north on the A37 and
turn right onto the A367 to
Stratton-on-the-Fosse, then
drive east on unclassified
roads through Holcombe
and Vobster to **Mells**.*

 **10**

9 SHEPTON MALLET

Nestling in a fold of the Mendip Hills, the historic market
town of Shepton Mallet dates back to Roman times.
From the 15th to the 17th centuries, it became a significant market and wool-trading centre, and many fine
examples of cloth merchants' houses still remain.

10 MELLS

A cluster of listed buildings, thatched cottages and an imposing 15th-century **church** make up the gorgeous village of Mells. The church has a lovely tower with diagonally-set pinnacles and a cemetery containing the grave of World War I poet Siegfried Sassoon. Mells is also known for its beautiful 14th-century manor house, seat of the Horner family whose ancestor supposedly gave rise to the childhood rhyme 'Little Jack Horner', after finding the deeds of the house hidden in a pie.

11 NUNNEY CASTLE

Dominating the attractive town of Nunney is this remarkable 14th-century moated castle built by John de la Mere after his return from the Hundred Years War. Designed to impress rather than defend, the fortified mansion borrows heavily from French style with closely spaced towers adorning a central townhouse. The castle suffered badly when it was attacked by Cromwellian forces during the Civil War, and the damage sustained eventually caused the complete collapse of the north wall.

12 BRUTON

It is worth stopping off at the sleepy town of Bruton for its lovely collection of buildings, which range from Jacobean almshouses to the wonderful Perpendicular church with its twin towers. A network of narrow alleyways or 'bartons' link Bruton with the River Brue and an unusual 16th-century dovecote that sits on a hill overlooking the town.

13 CADBURY CASTLE

The massive banks and ditches that surround the limestone hill at South Cadbury make it the largest hill fort in Somerset and certainly the kind of fortification that only a chieftain could afford to build. The site was probably first occupied about 5,000 years ago, but it is most famous for its connection to King Arthur. Although hotly disputed, many believe that this is the site of the legendary Camelot (Arthur's fortress and site of many of his most famous battles). A raised causeway called King Arthur's Hunting Track links the site to Glastonbury and adds credence to the claim. Either way, the impressive earthworks and stunning views make it an excellent spot for a walk and some fanciful musing.

14 FLEET AIR ARM MUSEUM

Highlights of this museum's large aircraft and military collection include the second prototype of Concorde and a simulated helicopter ride onto the flight deck of a 1970s aircraft carrier. The displays also cover aircraft from World War I, World War II and the Falklands, as well as up-to-date exhibitions on the latest airforce technology.

Head south on unclassified roads through Whatley to **Nunney Castle**. **11**

Take the A359 south from Nunney to **Bruton**. **12**

Continue south on the A359, then turn left onto the A303 and then quickly right to South Cadbury and **Cadbury Castle**. **13**

Return to the A303 and turn left, heading west through Sparkford. After Downhead, turn left onto the B3151 and follow signs left to the **Fleet Air Arm Museum**. **14**

Take the unclassified road just east of the museum, signposted for Bridge-hampton, to the A359, turn right and shortly after turn left on the B3148 to return to **Sherborne**.

WITH MORE TIME

Drive east onto the limestone ridge that forms the Mendip Hills *(left)* and you'll be rewarded with far-reaching views over the low-lying land below. The hills are littered with prehistoric earthworks, forts, barrows and the remains of the mining industry, and they offer great walks with a host of pretty villages and cosy pubs for excellent pit stops. By car, take a detour from Cheddar Gorge through **Compton Martin**, **West Harptree** and **East Harptree** and then on to **Chewton Mendip** before dropping down through unspoilt **Ebbor Gorge** to Wookey Hole.

Around Salisbury Plain: megaliths and mansions

Mysterious ancient monuments, picture-postcard villages, rolling chalk hills and numerous stately homes dot the landscape around Salisbury Plain, a sweeping plateau of grassland anchored by graceful Salisbury. Home to a spectacular cathedral and a labyrinth of medieval streets, Salisbury is the perfect starting point for a trip to enigmatic Stonehenge, and the ancient hill forts and romantic castle ruins that litter the area.

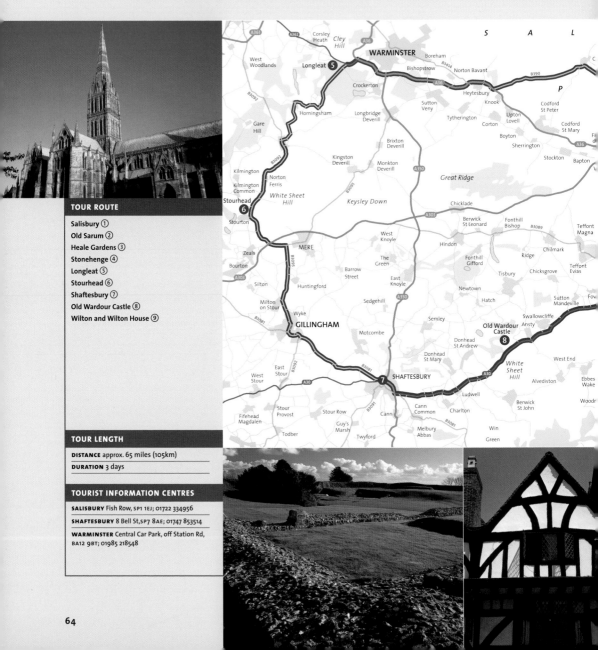

TOUR ROUTE

Salisbury ①
Old Sarum ②
Heale Gardens ③
Stonehenge ④
Longleat ⑤
Stourhead ⑥
Shaftesbury ⑦
Old Wardour Castle ⑧
Wilton and Wilton House ⑨

TOUR LENGTH

DISTANCE approx. 65 miles (105km)

DURATION 3 days

TOURIST INFORMATION CENTRES

SALISBURY Fish Row, SP1 1EJ; 01722 334956

SHAFTESBURY 8 Bell St, SP7 8AE; 01747 853514

WARMINSTER Central Car Park, off Station Rd, BA12 9BT; 01985 218548

1 SALISBURY

Dominated by the soaring spire of its majestic
cathedral, Salisbury is an atmospheric market town
boasting everything from medieval halls to half-
timbered Tudor townhouses. The jewel in its crown is
the stunning cathedral, a showpiece of Early English
Gothic style complete with pointed arches, flying
buttresses and a serene sense of light and space.
Inside, a host of interesting tombs line the austere
nave, including that of a boy-bishop. In the north aisle
you'll also find what is thought to be the oldest
working clock in the world, while behind the high altar
is the modern and striking *Prisoners of Conscience*
stained-glass window. The four central columns of the
nave are visibly buckled from the weight of the 125-m
spire (404ft), the tallest in Britain. Despite remedial
work, the tower leans precariously and a brass plate in
the floor of the nave measures the incline. Before
leaving the church via the tranquil cloister, visit the
octagonal Chapter House with its delicate fan vaulting
and one of only four original copies of the Magna Carta.

The **Cathedral Close** – lined with impressive buildings
and museums – is one of the largest and most
beautiful in the country. Look out for the 13th-century
Medieval Hall and the glorious Queen Anne-style
Mompesson House, used as a location in Ang Lee's film
Sense and Sensibility. Around the corner, the 15th-
century **St Thomas's Church** contains a bizarre
judgement day painting depicting naked bishops and
Christ sitting on a rainbow. Narrow lanes still bearing
their medieval names lead from here to the market
square where traders have convened since 1219; today,
markets are still held every Tuesday and Saturday.

2 OLD SARUM

First established in the Iron Age, the massive hill fort of
Old Sarum was continuously inhabited up until the
Middle Ages, when the pope decreed that its cathedral
could move down the hill and into the valley. All that
now remains on the site are the ruins of the castle,
cathedral and bishop's palace – and the stunning
views over the valley below.

*Take the A345 north out of
Salisbury for 2 miles and
follow the signs left
to Old Sarum.* **2**

*Continue north west on
unclassified roads via Lower
Woodford to Middle
Woodford and follow the
signs right to Heale Gardens.*
 **3**

⊕ *Continue on unclassified*
• *roads north from Middle*
• *Woodford to the A303, turn*
• *left and drive west until*
• *the road forks. Take the*
• *right fork onto the A360*
• *and* **Stonehenge** *is*
❹ *off to the left.*

3 HEALE GARDENS

A secret 17th-century hideaway of Charles II, Carolean Heale House is an imposing manor surrounded by fine gardens. Although the house is closed to the public, the beautiful gardens, partly laid out by Harold Peto in 1910, are worth a visit for the stunning herbaceous borders, shrub roses and the serene water garden with its Japanese tea-house and Nikko bridge.

4 STONEHENGE

Instantly recognisable and thronged with visitors, Stonehenge is Europe's most famous prehistoric monument. The mysterious stone circle was built by one of the world's earliest cultures, and work on the site began more than 5,000 years ago. Experts cannot agree on the original purpose of the stone circle, but the alignment of the inner horseshoe of stones with the rising sun at the summer solstice has lead to speculation that the site may have been used as a place of worship or ritual sacrifice or may even have been an astronomical clock. Everyone agrees, however, that the site was of incredible importance to the people of the time. Work continued on the site for 1,500 years, and the inner circle is made up of four-tonne megaliths that were dragged 250 miles from the Preseli Mountains in south Wales. The largest standing stones (each weighing about 50 tonnes) came from the Marlborough Downs, 20 miles away, and it is estimated some 600 men were needed to move each one.

Head north west along the A360 across the Salisbury Plain, then turn right onto the A36. After 6 miles turn left onto the A362 and shortly after follow the signs left to **Longleat**.

→ • • • • • • • • • • ❺

Clockwise from below:
Stonehenge; Wiltshire, Longleat safari park; the Pantheon and lake, Stourhead; Temple of Apollo, Stourhead

5 LONGLEAT

The first British stately home to open its doors to the paying public, Longleat has wholeheartedly embraced the concept of commercialism and makes for an absorbing day out. It now flaunts everything from a drive-through safari park to a Postman Pat village and the world's largest hedge maze, where the average person gets lost for an hour and a half. It is somewhat astonishing to see giraffes, rhinos and lions roaming the grounds landscaped by 'Capability' Brown. The beautiful, highly ornate Elizabethan house contains many fine treasures, as well as the erotic paintings of the famously eccentric owner, Lord Bath.

6 STOURHEAD

The grand Palladian mansion at Stourhead is filled with Chippendale furniture and paintings by the Old Masters, and yet it pales in comparison to the gorgeous gardens that surround it. Laid out between 1741 and 1780, the landscaped grounds are heaving with neoclassical monuments and follies set around a large lake. A lakeside path meanders through mature growths of exotic trees and over ornamental bridges giving constantly changing views of the monuments and their rippling reflections. A longer walk leads to King Alfred's Tower, a 50m-high brick folly (165ft) affording great views over the estate and surrounding countryside.

Head south on unclassified roads via Horningsham to the B3092. Turn left and drive south for 4 miles, then follow the signs right to Stourhead. 6

Continue south on the B3092 over the junction with the A303 and join the B3095 south through Gillingham and left onto the B3081 to Shaftesbury.

 7

⬇ *Take the A350 south and turn left onto the A30. Head east for 6 miles until the signposted turning on the*
❽ *left to Old Wardour Castle.*

Continue travelling north east on the A30 to Wilton. Wilton House is signposted to the right off the round-about on Minster Street.

→ • • • • • • • • • • ❾

7 SHAFTESBURY

Lording it over the surrounding plains, the town of Shaftesbury is perched on an outcrop of sandstone and offers brilliant views over Blackmore Vale. At the height of its fortunes, the town boasted a castle, 12 churches and four market crosses. Its most famous attraction today is charming **Gold Hill**, a steep, curving cobbled street of thatched cottages used as a film location in *Far from the Madding Crowd* and in the classic Hovis bread advert. To see inside one of the quaint cottages pop into the **Shaftesbury Town Museum**, where you can also gain insight on the history of the town and its abbey. Once the richest nunnery in England, **Shaftesbury Abbey** was founded by Alfred the Great in AD888 and razed by Henry VIII 650 years later. Today only the foundations remain.

8 OLD WARDOUR CASTLE

One of the most romantic ruins in England, Old Wardour Castle has a stunning lakeside setting and a bloody, tormented past. Made famous by Kevin Costner's *Robin Hood: Prince of Thieves*, the unique six-sided castle was originally built by Lord Lovel in the 14th century and took its inspiration from French chateaux. By the early 17th century, it was the royalist Arundell family who ruled the roost, and in 1643 some 1,300 advancing Parliamentarians besieged the castle with only Lady Blanche Arundell and 25 men to defend it. They managed to hold out for almost one month before the castle was captured; the lady of the house was imprisoned and later executed. Six months on, a countersiege began, which ended only when gunpowder mines under the castle exploded and destroyed it beyond repair. The ruined castle soon became a backdrop for a new house, but to this day Lady Arundell's ghost is said to wander the castle ruins at twilight.

WOODFORD VALLEY TRAIL

North of Salisbury lies the Woodford Valley, renowned for its charming, riverside thatched cottages. Though it makes a pleasant drive, it is best appreciated on foot, and there is an easy, circular waymarked route that wanders through the valley from Upper Woodford, taking about three hours to complete. Head north from the Bridge Inn in **Upper Woodford** through a small wood and along the river to the picturesque villages of **Great Durnford** and **Wilsford**. From here the trail leads to **Normanton Down** where you can explore ancient burial mounds and take in fabulous views over Stonehenge. The route then circles back to Upper Woodford. A second, shorter trail starts in **Lower Woodford** and explores the lower river valley passing thatched homes, quaint estate cottages and a manor house en route.

Clockwise from far left:
Gold Hill, Shaftesbury;
Cube Room, Wilton House;
Palladian bridge,
Wilton House

9 WILTON AND WILTON HOUSE

Renowned for its carpet industry, the quaint market town of **Wilton** was once the ancient capital of Wessex and today makes a pleasant stopping-off point for its Georgian houses, riverside walk and numerous antique shops. Its real gem, however, is the exquisite **Wilton House**, home to the earls of Pembroke since 1542. The house was rebuilt by Indigo Jones after a major fire in 1647, and its sumptuous interiors feature elaborate plasterwork, ornate ceilings and a host of paintings by Van Dyck, Rembrandt, Poussin and Tintoretto. The beautiful gardens have attracted numerous film-makers: scenes from *The Madness of King George* and *Mrs Brown* were shot here, and the stunning Double Cube Room appears as the ballroom in *Sense and Sensibility*.

Leave Wilton heading
east on the A36 to
return to **Salisbury**.

WITH MORE TIME

If time permits, extend your route north via the sleepy village of **Tilshead** to look at its distinctive flint and stone buildings. Continue to **Edington**, where the priory – all that is left of a 14th-century Augustinian monastery – beautifully exemplifies the architectural transition from Decorated to Perpendicular style, with an unusual two-storey porch, medieval marble floors, Victorian mosaics and fine plaster ceilings. To the west in Bratton, you can stretch your legs on a steep climb to the **Westbury White Horse** *(left)*, which dates from the 18th century.

Bath: an elegant legacy of times past

Cultivated and ever-so elite, Bath still evokes a certain 18th-century exclusivity. Expensive galleries, chi-chi boutiques, alluring antique shops and fine restaurants rub shoulders with fascinating museums and architectural gems. It is a wonderful place to simply stroll around, to soak up the atmosphere and to lose oneself in a Georgian high society daydream.

TOUR LOCATIONS

Royal Baths ①
Thermae Bath Spa & Hetling Pump Room ②
Pump Room ③
Bath Abbey ④
Sally Lunn's House ⑤
No.1 Royal Crescent ⑥
Assembly Rooms ⑦
Building of Bath Museum ⑧
Jane Austen Centre ⑨
Victoria Art Gallery ⑩
Pulteney Bridge ⑪
Holburne Museum of Art ⑫
Bath Aqua Theatre of Glass ⑬
Theatre Royal ⑭

TOUR LENGTH

DISTANCE With the exception of The Holburne Museum of Art, all Bath's attractions are in the city centre and within easy walking distance of each other. The proximity of each attraction means that it is possible to take the tour in any particular order.

DURATION 1–2 days

TOURIST INFORMATION CENTRES

BATH Abbey Chambers, Abbey Church Yard, ba1 1ly; 0906 711 2000

Clockwise from far left:
Bath Abbey; detail, Roman
Baths; Roman Baths;
Pulteney Bridge and River
Avon; outdoor pool,
Thermae Bath Spa

BATHWICK

Holburne
Museum of Art
13

Sydney
Gardens

Pavilion

Bowling
Green

Recreation
Ground

Bath Sport &
Leisure Centre

North Parade
Cricket Ground

Pavilion

Bath Cricket
Club

DOLEMEADS

WIDCOMBE

1 ROMAN BATHS

The city has traded on the presence of Britain's only hot
springs since Celtic times, but it was the Romans who
had the engineering skills to create the great bathing
complex you see today. Britain's only hot springs drew
the Romans to Bath, and the magnificent remains of
their bathing complex are now one of England's most
popular attractions. The baths fell into decline after the
downfall of the Roman Empire, but a visit by Queen
Anne sealed their status as the fashionable place to
'take the cure' in the 18th century. The grandiose main
pool or Great Bath is surrounded by statues of famous
Roman emperors and governors and is overlooked by a
gallery that was added in Victorian times. Every day,
around one million litres (220,000 gallons) of hot water
flows through the complex from the Sacred Spring, and
fills the pools. The Romans believed the surging water
was the work of the gods, and a built a temple to
honour the local goddess, Sulis Minerva, on the site. The
Roman Baths complex is below the modern street level
and an audio guide takes you through the four main
features: the Sacred Spring, the Roman Temple, the
Roman bath house and finds from Roman Bath. On
your journey you can inspect the warren of underground
passages and chambers, see the sophisticated pumping
and draining systems created by the Roman engineers,
and study the fascinating displays of artefacts found on
the site which give an intriguing insight into the lives
of the Romans who lived and worked in the area.

2 THERMAE BATH SPA
& HETLING PUMP ROOM

Two other baths, the Cross Bath and the Hot Bath, were
connected to the main baths by a covered walkway and
today they have been incorporated into the magnificent
Thermae Bath Spa. Here you can gaze skywards as you
laze in the rooftop pool and take advantage of state-of-
the-art spa facilities. If you don't have the time for such
indulgence, visit the Spa Visitor Centre in the Hetling
Pump Room where displays and exhibits unfold the
story, from the founding of Roman Bath to the recent
revival of Bath's spa quarter. At the on-site drinking
fountain, the unique flavour of the waters can be sampled.

Clockwise from above:
Royal Crescent; stained glass
windows, Bath Abbey; The
Jane Austen Centre; The
Victoria Art Gallery; Sally
Lunn's House

3 PUMP ROOM

Nearby, is the late 18th-century Pump Room. For more
than two centuries, this lay at the centre of Bath's high
society – as both the city's and the country's luminaries
arrived in their droves to sample the purifying qualities
of its spa water. The hall now houses a restaurant where
the Pump Room Trio play music daily throughout the year.

4 BATH ABBEY

When you have finished relaxing in the ancient Pump
Room surroundings, it is time to visit Bath Abbey. This
imposing structure was built on the former site of a
Norman cathedral and is a superlative example of
Perpendicular style, with slender pillars and soaring
vertical lines. The present abbey was begun in 1499,
after a dream inspired the then bishop, Oliver King, to
raze the ruined church and build a monument to the
glory of God. The west front depicts his vision of angels
climbing up a ladder to heaven. Inside, elaborate
monuments and memorials, including the tomb of the
city's Victorian society dandy, Beau Nash, line a nave
illuminated by magnificent stained-glass windows and
decorated with breathtaking fan vaulting.

5 SALLY LUNN'S HOUSE

Nearby, you will find Sally Lunn's House. It was built in
1483, is the oldest house in Bath and the home of a
globally renowned light semi-sweet bread called the
Sally Lunn Bun. You can still sample the buns here, see
the building's Medieval and Roman foundations and
survey the original kitchens, as used by Sally Lunn over
300 years ago.

6 NO.1 ROYAL CRESCENT

Bath's heyday was as a spa resort in the 18th century
when artists, writers and aristocrats flocked here to be a
part of fashionable society. Today, Bath boasts more than
5,000 listed buildings and is a World Heritage Site. The
gracious, sweeping, honey-coloured curves of the **Circus**
and the **Royal Crescent** are the elegant highlights of a
city heaving with Palladian mansions and stunning
townhouses. To peek inside one of the city's treasures
visit No. 1 Royal Crescent, which has been restored to its
original glory. Built between 1767 and 1774, it is rightly
considered to be one of the finest examples of 18th-
century urban architecture in England

7 ASSEMBLY ROOMS

The Assembly Rooms were purpose-built in the 18th-
century for a form of entertainment called an 'assembly'.
This involved a large number of guests meeting to drink
tea, play cards, dance and listen to music. Today they

house the **Museum of Costume**, which is devoted to fashion from the late 16th century to the present day. It contains more than 30,000 items in its collection, hosts regular special exhibitions and possesses one of the world's finest collections of fashionable dress.

8 BUILDING OF BATH MUSEUM

To find out more about the city's architecture, visit the Building of Bath Museum which, using a series of maps, models, paintings and reconstructions, explains how this magnificent city evolved.

9 BATH AQUA THEATRE OF GLASS

Back in the heart of the city's artisan quarter you can watch the ancient craft of free blown and stained glass making in a dramatic working environment at Bath Aqua Theatre of Glass .

10 JANE AUSTEN CENTRE

Many of Bath's famous buildings are mentioned in Jane Austen's novels, in particular *Northanger Abbey* and *Persuasion*. To gain insight into the Bath of her time, visit The Jane Austen Centre where you can see period prints and displays on her personal life.

11 VICTORIA ART GALLERY

Bath is also a great centre for the arts. The Victoria Art Gallery houses oil paintings that date from the 15th to the 20th century. Its collection includes works by painters who were active in the Bath area, such as Gainsborough, Sickert and Turner.

12 PULTENEY BRIDGE

Pulteney Bridge was built in the Italiante style and is lined with shops and presides over the beautiful V-shaped weir on the River Avon below.

13 HOLBURNE MUSEUM OF ART

Across Pulteney Bridge and a little away from the city centre you'll find the Holburne Museum of Art. It is housed in an 18th-century building set in beautiful parkland and is home to a stunning collection of furniture, porcelain and paintings, including important works by Gainsborough, Guardi, Stubbs and Turner.

14 THEATRE ROYAL

Finally, at the end of your tour, perhaps it is time to experience the city's dramatic arts. Take in a play or go behind the scenes on a stage tour of The Theatre Royal , which is one of the country's oldest working theatres.

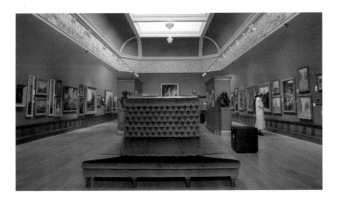

Gazetteer

Along the rugged Cornish coast

The Abbey Garden and Valhalla Collection
Tresco, Isles of Scilly TR24 OQQ
Tel: 01720 424105
www.tresco.co.uk

Barbara Hepworth Museum & Sculpture Garden
Barnoon Hill, St Ives TR26 1AD
Tel: 01736 796226
www.tate.org.uk

Geevor Tin Mine
Pendeen, Penzance TR19 7EW
Tel: 01736 788662
www.sennen-cove.com

Glendurgan Garden
Mawnan Smith, nr Falmouth TR11 5JZ
Tel: 01326 250906
www.nationaltrust.org.uk

The Leach Pottery
Higher Stennack, St Ives TR26 2HE
Tel: 01736 796398
www.leachpottery.com

Marazion Marsh Nature Reserve
nr Penzance
Tel: 01736 711682
www.rspb.org.uk

The Minack Theatre Visitor Centre
Porthcurno, Penzance TR19 6JU
Tel: 01736 810181
www.minack.com

National Maritime Museum Cornwall
Discovery Quay, Falmouth TR11 3QY
Tel: 01326 313 388
www.nmmc.co.uk

The National Seal Sanctuary
Gweek, nr Helston TR12 6UG
Tel: 01326 221361
www.sealsanctuary.co.uk

Newlyn Art Gallery
24 New Road, Newlyn TR18 5PZ
Tel: 01736 363715
www.newlynartgallery.co.uk

Pendennis Castle
Falmouth
Tel: 01326 316594
www.english-heritage.org

Penlee House Gallery and Museum
Morrab Road, Penzance TR18 4HE
Tel: 01736 363625
www.penleehouse.org.uk

Porthcurno Telegraph Museum
Eastern House, Porthcurno TR19 6JX
Tel: 01736 810966
www.porthcurno.org.uk

Royal Cornwall Museum
River Street, Truro TR1 2SJ
Tel: 01872 272205
www.royalcornwallmuseum.org.uk

St Mawes Castle
St Mawes
01326 270526
www.english-heritage.org.uk

St Ives Society of Artists
Norway Square, St Ives TR26 1NA
Tel: 01736 795582
www.stivessocietyofartists.com

St Michael's Mount
Marazion, Pensance TR17 OEF
Tel: 01736 710507
www.nationaltrust.org.uk

Tate St Ives
Porthmeor Beach, St Ives TR26 1TG
Tel: 01736 796226
www.tate.org.uk

Trebah Garden
Mawnan Smith, nr Falmouth TR11 5JZ
Tel: 01326 250448
www.trebahgarden.co.uk

Trelissick Garden
Feock, nr Truro TR3 6QL
Tel: 01872 862090
www.nationaltrust.org.uk

Truro Cathedral
14 St Mary's Street, Truro TR1 2AF
Tel: 01872 276782
www.trurocathedral.org.uk

Wayside Folk Museum
Zennor TR26 3DA
Tel: 01736 796945
www.cornwall-online.co.uk

The wilds of Bodmin Moor

Bodmin Jail
Berrycoombe Road, Bodmin PL31 2NR
Tel: 01208 76292
www.cornwall-online.co.uk

Bodmin Town Museum
Mount Folly, Bodmin PL31 2HQ
Tel: 01208 77067
www.north-cornwall.com

The Courtroom Experience
Shire Hall, Mount Folly, Bodmin PL31 2DQ
Tel: 01208 76616
www.bodminmoor.co.uk

Daphne du Maurier's Smuggler's Museum at Jamaica Inn
Bolventor, Launceston PL15 7TS
Tel: 01566 86838
www.jamaicainn.co.uk**

Eden Project
Bodelva, St Austell PL24 2SG
Tel: 01726 811911
www.edenproject.com

The John Betjeman Centre
Southern Way, Wadebridge PL27 7BX
Tel: 01208 812392

Lanhydrock
nr Bodmin PL30 5AD
Tel: 01208 265950
www.nationaltrust.org.uk

The Lost Gardens of Heligan
Pentewan, St Austell PL26 6EN
Tel: 01726 845100
www.heligan.com

Military Museum
The Keep, Bodmin PL31 1EG
Tel: 01208 72810
www.cornwalltouristboard.co.uk

The Minions Heritage Centre
Minions, Liskeard PL14 5LJ
Tel: 01579 362350
www.caradon.gov.uk

The Museum of Witchcraft
The Harbour, Boscastle PL35 OHD
Tel: 01840 250111
www.museumofwitchcraft.com

National Lobster Hatchery
South Quay, Padstow PL28 8BL
Tel: 01841 533877
www.chycor.co.uk

Pencarrow House and Gardens
Bodmin PL30 3AG
Tel: 01208 841369
www.pencarrow.co.uk

Prideaux Place
Padstow PL28 8RP
Tel: 01841 532411
www.prideauxplace.co.uk

St Neot Pottery
The Old Chapel, St Neot, Liskeard PL14 6NL
Tel: 01579 320216
www.caradon.gov.uk

Tintagel Castle
Tintagel
Tel: 01840 770328
www.english-heritage.org.uk

Tintagel Old Post Office
Fore Street, Tintagel PL34 0DB
Tel: 01840 770024
www.nationaltrust.org.uk

Beneath Dartmoor's craggy heights

Buckland Abbey
Yelverton PL20 6EY
Tel: 01822 853607
www.nationaltrust.org.uk

The Cardew Teapottery
Newton Road, Bovey Tracey TQ13 9DX
Tel: 01626 832172
www.cardewdesign.com

Castle Drogo
Drewsteignton, nr Exeter EX6 6PB
Tel: 01647 433306
www.nationaltrust.org.uk

Cotehele
St Dominick, nr Saltash PL12 6TA
01579 352739
www.nationaltrust.org.uk

Cotehele Quay Museum
Cotehele Quay, St Dominick,
Saltash PL12 6TA.
Tel: 01579 350830
www.tamarvalley.org.uk

The Garden House
Buckland Monachorum,
Yelverton PL20 7LQ
Tel: 01822 854769
www.thegardenhouse.org.uk

House of Marbles
The Old Pottery, Pottery Road
Bovey Tracey TQ13 9DS
Tel: 01626 835358
www.houseofmarbles.com

Morwellham Quay
Nr Tavistock PL19 8JL
Tel: 01822 832766
www.morwhellam-quay.co.uk

Mount Edgcumbe House
Cremyll, Torpoint PL10 1HZ
Tel: 01752 822236
www.mountedgcumbe.gov.uk

Plymouth Dome
Hoe Road, Plymouth PL1 2NZ
Tel: 01752 603300
www.plymouthdome.info

Riverside Mill
Bovey Tracey TQ13 9AF
Tel: 01626 832223
www.boveytracey.gov.uk

The English Riviera and the sleepy South Hams

Berry Pomeroy Castle
nr Totnes
Tel: 01803 866 618
www.english-heritage.org.uk

Brixham Heritage Museum
Bolton Cross, Brixham TQ5 8LZ
Tel: 01803 856267
www.devonmuseums.net

Cockington Court Craft Centre
Cockington, Torquay TQ2 6XA
Tel: 01803 606035
www.theenglishriviera.co.uk

Coleton Fishacre
Coleton, Kingswear, Dartmouth TQ6 0EQ
Tel: 01803 752466
www.nationaltrust.org.uk

Cookworthy Museum
The Old Grammar School
108 Fore Street, Kingsbridge TQ7 1AW
Tel: 01548 853235
www.devonmuseums.net

Dart Valley Light Railway
Queens Park Station, Torbay Road,
Paignton TQ4 6AF
Tel: 01803 555872
www.torbay.gov.uk

Dartmouth Castle
Dartmouth
Tel: 01803 833588
www.english-heritage.org.uk

Elizabethan Museum
70 Fore Street, Totnes TQ9 5RU
Tel: 01803 863821
www.devonmuseums.net

Exeter Cathedral
Exeter EX1 1HS
Tel: 01392 285983
www.exeter-cathedral.org.uk

Golden Hind
Brixham Harbour, Brixham
Tel: 01803 856223
www.goldenhind.co.uk

Greenway
Greenway Road, Galmpton,
nr Brixham TQ5 0ES
Tel: 01803 842382
www.nationaltrust.org.uk

The Guildhall
Ramparts Walk, Totnes TQ9 5QH
Tel: 01803 862147
www.devon-online.com

Kents Cavern
Cavern House, Ilsham Road,
Torquay TQ1 2JF
Tel: 01803 215136
www.kents-cavern.co.uk

Living Coasts
Torquay Harbourside, Beacon Quay
Torquay TQ1 2BG
Tel: 01803 202499
www.livingcoasts.org.uk

Overbeck's Museum & Garden
Sharpitor, Salcombe TQ8 8LW
Tel: 01548 842893
www.nationaltrust.org.uk

**Royal Albert Memorial Museum and
Art Gallery**
Queen Street, Exeter EX4 3RX
Tel: 01392 665858
www.exeter.gov.uk

Slapton Ley National Nature Reserve
Slapton, Kingsbridge TQ7 2QP
Tel: 01548 580685
www.slnnr.org.uk

Torquay Museum
529 Babbacombe Road, Torquay TQ1 1HG
Tel: 01803 293275
www.torquaymuseum.org

Torre Abbey Historic House and Gallery
The King's Drive, Torquay TQ2 5JE
Tel: 01803 293593
www.torre-abbey.org.uk

Rural backwaters of North Devon

Arlington Court
Arlington, nr Barnstaple EX31 4LP
Tel: 01271 850296
www.nationaltrust.org.uk

Barnstaple Heritage Centre
Queen Anne's Walk, The Strand
Barnstaple EX31 1EU
Tel: 01271 373003
www.devonmuseums.net

The Burton Art Gallery and Museum
Kingsley Road, Bideford EX39 2QQ
Tel: 01237 471455
www.burtonartgallery.co.uk

Cobbaton Combat Collection
Chittlehampton, Umberleigh EX37 9RZ
Tel: 01769 540740
www.cobbatoncombat.co.uk

Dartington Crystal Visitor Centre
Torrington EX38 7AN
Tel: 01805 626242
www.dartington.co.uk

Hartland Abbey
Hartland, Bideford EX39 6DT
Tel: 01237 441264/234
www.hartlandabbey.com

Hartland Quay Museum
Hartland, nr Bideford EX39 6DU
Tel: 01288 331353
www.devonheritage.com

Kingsley Museum
Clovelly, Bideford EX39 5SY
Tel: 01237 431781
www.north-cornwall.com

Marwood Hill Gardens
Barnstaple EX31 4EB
Tel: 01271 342528
www.marwoodhillgarden.co.uk

Museum of Barnstaple and North Devon
The Square, Barnstaple EX32 8LN
Tel: 01271 346747
www.devonmuseums.net

North Devon Maritime Museum
Odun Road, Appledore, Bideford EX39 1PT
Tel: 01237 422064
www.devonmuseums.net

Rosemoor
Great Torrington EX38 8PH
Tel: 01805 624067
www.rhs.org.uk

Tapeley Park
Instow, Bideford EX39 4NT
Tel: 01271 342558
www.tapeleypark.com

Torrington 1646
Castle Hill, South Street,
Great Torrington EX38 8AA
Tel: 01805 626146
www.torrington-1646.co.uk

Watermouth Castle
Berrynarbor, Ilfracombe EX34 9SL
Tel: 01271 864474
www.watermouthcastle.com

THE MAGIC OF EXMOOR

Cothay Manor and Gardens
Greenham, Nr Wellington TA21 0JR
Tel: 01823 672283
www.somerset.gov.uk
Dunster Castle
Dunster, nr Minehead TA24 6SL
Tel: 01643 823004
www.nationaltrust.org.uk

Dunster Working Watermill
Mill Lane, Dunster, nr Minehead TA24 6SW
Tel: 01643 821759
www.nationaltrust.org.uk

Exmoor National Park Authority
Exmoor House, Dulverton TA22 9HL
Tel: 01398 323665
www.exmoor-nationalpark.gov.uk

Hestercombe Gardens
Cheddon Fitzpaine, Taunton TA2 8LG
Tel: 01823 413923
www.hestercombegardens.com

Knightshayes Court
Bolham, Tiverton EX16 7RQ
Tel: 01884 254665
www.nationaltrust.org.uk

Lyn and Exmoor Museum
Market St, Lynton EX35 6HJ
Tel: 01598 752317
www.devonmuseums.net

Lynton and Lynmouth Cliff Railway
Bottom Station, The Esplanade, Lynmouth
Tel: 01598 753486
www.cliffrailwaylynton.co.uk

The West Somerset Railway
The Railway Station, Minehead TA24 5BG
Tel: 01643 704996
www.west-somerset-railway.co.uk

INLAND FROM THE JURASSIC COAST

Barrington Court
Barrington, nr Ilminster TA19 0NQ
Tel: 01460 242614
www.nationaltrust.org.uk

Beer Quarry Caves
Quarry Lane, Beer, nr Seaton
Tel: 01297 680282
www.eastdevon.net

Branscombe
Branscombe, Seaton EX12 3DB
Tel: 01297 680333 (Old Bakery); 01392
881691 (Manor Mill); 01297 680481 (Forge)
www.nationaltrust.org.uk

Bridport Museum
South Street, Bridport DT6 3NR
Tel: 01308 422116
www.bridportmuseum.co.uk

Brown and Forrest
Bowdens Farm, Hambridge TA10 0BP
Tel: 01458 250875
www.smokedeel.co.uk

Charmouth Heritage Coast Centre
Lower Sea Lane, Charmouth DT6 6LL
Tel: 01297 560772
www.charmouth.org

Dinosaurland
Coombe Street, Lyme Regis DT7 3PY
Tel: 01297 443541
www.dinosaurland.co.uk

East Lambrook Manor Gardens
South Petherton TA13 5HH
Tel: 01460 240328
www.eastlambrook.co.uk

Forde Abbey
Chard TA20 4LU
Tel: 01460 220231
www.fordeabbey.co.uk

Forde Abbey Fruit Farm
Chard TA20 4LU
Tel: 01460 30460
www.somerset.gov.uk

The Heritage Centre
Market Square, Crewkerne TA18 7JU
Tel: 01460 77079
www.somerset.gov.uk

Lyme Regis Philpot Museum
Bridge Street, Lyme Regis DT7 3QA
Tel: 01297 443370
www.jurassiccoast.com

Norman Lockyer Observatory
Salcombe Hill, Sidmouth EX10 0NY
www.projects.ex.ac.uk

Perry's Cider
Dowlish Wake, Ilminster TA19 0NY
Tel: 01460 55195
www.perryscider.co.uk

Seaton Tramway
Riverside Depot, Harbour Road,
Seaton EX12 2NQ
Tel: 01297 20375
www.tram.co.uk

**The Somerset Cider Brandy Company Ltd
& Burrow Hill Cider**
Pass Vale Farm, Burrow Hill, Kingsbury
Episcopi Martock TA12 5BU
Tel: 01460 240782
www.ciderbrandy.co.uk

THOMAS HARDY'S DORSET

Abbotsbury Sub-Tropical Gardens
Bullers Way, Abbotsbury DT3 4LA
Tel: 01305 871387
www.abbotsbury-tourism.co.uk

Abbotsbury Swannery
New Barn Road, Abbotsbury DT3 4JG
Tel: 01305 871858
www.abbotsbury-tourism.co.uk

Abbotsbury Tithe Barn
New Barn Road, Abbotsbury DT3 4JG
Tel: 01305 871817
www.abbotsbury-tourism.co.uk

Athelhampton House & Garden
Athelhampton, Dorchester DT2 7LG
Tel: 01305 848363
www.athelhampton.co.uk

The Blue Pool
Furzebrook, nr Wareham BH20 5AT
Tel: 01929 551408
www.blue.pool.users.btopenworld.com

Clouds Hill
Wareham, BH20 7NQ
Tel: 01929 405616
www.nationaltrust.org.uk

Corfe Castle
The Square, Corfe Castle BH20 5EZ
Tel: 01929 481294
www.nationaltrust.org.uk

Dorset County Museum
High West Street, Dorchester DT1 1XA
Tel: 01305 262735
www.dorsetcountymuseum.org

Durlston Country Park
Lighthouse Road, Swanage BH19 2JL
Tel: 01929 424443
www.durlston.co.uk

Hardy's Cottage
Higher Bockhampton, nr Dorchester DT2
8QJ
Tel: 01305 262366
www.nationaltrust.org.uk

Kingston Lacy
Wimborne Minster BH21 4EA
Tel: 01202 880413
www.nationaltrust.org.uk

Lulworth Heritage Centre
Main Road, Lulworth BH20 5QS
Tel: 01929 400587
www.lulworth.com

Max Gate
Alington Avenue, Dorchester DT1 2AA
Tel: 01305 262538
www.nationaltrust.org.uk

Old Crown Court and Cells
Stratton House, High West Street
Dorchester DT1 1UZ
Tel: 01305 252241
www.westdorset.com

The Roman Town House
Colliton Park, Dorchester
Tel: 01305 228507
www.visit-dorchester.co.uk

Swanage Railway
Station House, Swanage BH19 1HB
Tel: 01929 425800
www.swanagerailway.co.uk

Tolpuddle Martyrs Museum
Tolpuddle, Dorchester DT2 7EH
Tel: 01305 848 237
www.tolpuddlemartyrs.org.uk

Wimborne Minster
High Street, Wimborne BH21 1HT
Tel: 01202 884753
www.wimborneminster.org.uk

ON THE TRAIL OF KING ARTHUR

Bishops' Palace
Wells BA5 2PD
Tel: 01749 678691
www.bishopspalacewells.co.uk

Cadbury Castle
South Cadbury BA22 7HA

Chalice Well
Chilkwell Street, Glastonbury BA6 8DD
Tel: 01458 831154
www.chalicewell.org.uk

Cheddar Caves and Gorge
Cheddar BS27 3QF
Tel: 01934 742343
www.cheddarcaves.co.uk

Clarks Village
Farm Road, Street BA16 0BB
Tel: 01458 840064
www.clarksvillage.co.uk

Fleet Air Arm Museum
Yeovilton, nr Ilchester BA22 8HT
Tel: 01935 840565
www.fleetairarm.com

Glastonbury Abbey
Magdalene Street, Glastonbury BA6 9EL
Tel: 01458 832267
www.glastonburyabbey.com

Glastonbury Tor
nr Glastonbury
Tel: 01985 843600
www.nationaltrust.org.uk

Montacute House
Montacute TA15 6XP
Tel: 01935 823289
www.nationaltrust.org.uk

Sherborne Abbey
Sherborne DT9 3LQ
Tel: 01935 812452
www.sherborneabbey.com

Sherborne Castle
Cheap Street, Sherborne DT9 3PY
Tel: 01935 813182
www.sherbornecastle.com

Sherborne House
Newland, Sherborne DT9 3JG
Tel: 01935 816426
www.sherbornehouse.org.uk

Sherborne Old Castle
Sherborne
Tel: 01935 812730
www.english-heritage.org.uk

Sherborne Museum
Abbey Gate House, Sherborne DT9 3BP
Tel: 01935 812252
www.westdorset.com

Wells Cathedral
Wells BA5 2UE
Tel: 01749 674433
www.wellscathedral.org.uk

Wookey Hole Caves
Wells BA5 1BB
Tel: 01749 672243
www.wookey.co.uk

AROUND SALISBURY PLAIN: MEGALITHS AND MANSIONS

Heale Gardens
Middle Woodford, Salisbury SP4 6NT
Tel: 01722 782504
www.visitwiltshire.co.uk

Longleat
Warminster BA12 7NW
Tel: 01985 844400
www.longleat.co.uk

The Medieval Hall
Sarum St Michael, West Walk
Cathedral Close, Salisbury SP1 2EY
Tel: 01722 412472
www.medieval-hall.co.uk

Mompesson House
The Close, Salisbury SP1 2EL
Tel: 01722 420980
www.nationaltrust.org.uk

Old Sarum
Castle Road, Salisbury SP1 3SD
Tel: 01722 335398
www.english-heritage.org.uk

Old Wardour Castle
nr Tisbury SP3 6RR
Tel: 01747 870487
www.english-heritage.org.uk

Salisbury Cathedral
Salisbury SP1 2EF
Tel: 01722 555 121
www.salisburycathedral.org.uk

Shaftesbury Abbey Museum & Garden
Park Walk, Shaftesbury SP7 8JR
Tel: 01747 852910
www.shaftesburyabbey.co.uk

Shaftesbury Town Museum
1 Gold Hill, Shaftesbury SP7 8JW
Tel: 01747 852157
www.shaftesburydorset.com

Stonehenge
nr Amesbury
Tel: 0870 333 118
www.english-heritage.org.uk

Stourhead
Stourton, Warminster BA12 6QD
Tel: 01747 841152
www.nationaltrust.org.uk

Wilton House
Wilton, Salisbury SP2 0BJ
Tel: 01722 746714
www.wiltonhouse.co.uk

BATH: ELEGANT
LEGACY OF TIMES PAST

Bath Abbey
Bath BA1 1LT
Tel: 01225 422462
www.bathabbey.org

Bath Assembly Rooms
Bennett Street, Bath BA1 2QH
Tel: 01225 477752
www.nationaltrust.org.uk

Bath Aqua Theatre of Glass
1-2 Orange Grove, Bath BA1 5LW
Tel: 01225 311183
www.bathaquaglass.com

Building of Bath Museum
The Vineyards, Bath BA1 5NA
Tel: 01225 333895
www.bath-preservation-trust.org.uk

Holburne Museum of Art
Great Pulteney Street, Bath BA2 4DB
Tel: 01225 466669
www.bath.ac.uk

Jane Austen Centre
40 Gay Street, Queens Square, Bath BA1 2NT
Tel: 01225 443000
www.janeausten.co.uk

Museum of Costume
Assembly Rooms, Bennett Street
Bath BA1 2QH
Tel: 01225 477173
www.museumofcostume.co.uk

No 1 Royal Crescent
Bath BA1 2LR
Tel: 01225 428126
www.bath-preservation-trust.org.uk

Pump Room
Stall Street, Bath BA1 1LZ
Tel: 01225 477785
www.bath-preservation-trust.org

Roman Baths
Bath BA1 1LZ
Tel: 01225 477785
www.romanbaths.co.uk

Sally Lunn's House
4 North Parade Passage, Bath BA1 1NX
Tel: 01225 461634
www.sallylunns.co.uk

Theatre Royal
Sawclose, Bath BA1 1ET
Tel: 01225 448844
www.theatreroyal.org.uk

Thermae Bath Spa
The Hetling Pump Room, Hot Bath Street
Bath BA1 1SJ
Tel: 01225 331234
www.thermaebathspa.com

Victoria Art Gallery
Bridge Street, Bath BA2 4AT
Tel: 01225 477232
www.victoriagal.org.uk

Index

Credits

t = top; tl = top left; top centre = tc; top right = tr; centre = c; centre above = ca; centre below = cb; bottom = b; bottom left = bl; bottom centre = bc; bottom right = br

VisitBritain would like to thank the following for their assistance with photographic material for this publication:
Bath Tourism Plus 73br; **Devon Tourism** 24b, 25b, 36b, 38b, 39; **Fleet Air Museum** 63c; **Somerset Tourism** 44–5c, 46b, 51t; **Thermae Bath Spa/Matt Cardy** 3b, 70bc

All remaining photographs including jacket images have been sourced from VisitBritain's online picture library (www.britainonview.com), with credits to:
Helen Harrison 40b; **Nigel Hicks** 33t, 35t, 47t; **Doug McKinley** 6–7; **Ingrid Rasmussen** 72br; **David Sellman** 72t; **Roger Westlake** 31t; **Robert Westwood** 41t, 64bl

Map on pages 70–71 courtesy of Bath Tourism Plus, official marketing organisation for the City of Bath, England, www.visitbath.co.uk

Design: Anthony Limerick, Clare Thorpe, Janis Utton
Editorial: Naomi Peck, Debbie Woska
Picture Research: Rebecca Shoben
Publishing: Jane Collinson, Edward Farrow

VEGETABLE BURGERS

Serves 3–4

6 carrots, cleaned and finely
  chopped
4 small onions, peeled and chopped
225g (8oz) yellow split peas,
  soaked and simmered until soft
1 tbsp parsley, chopped
1 clove garlic
Salt and pepper
2 small eggs, beaten
110g (4oz) fine dry bread crumbs
2 tbsp oil

Bring carrots and onions to the boil, then simmer until softened. Drain and mash carrots and onions, add yellow peas, chopped parsley and garlic, binding with beaten egg. Make into round burger shapes and dip in egg and breadcrumbs, then heat oil in large frying pan and fry the burgers until they are crisp and brown. These go well with pureed peas or brussels sprouts and creamed potatoes.

CHEESE AND CELERY PIE

Serves 4

450g (1lb) short crust pastry
225g (8oz) Cheddar cheese,
  coarsely grated
3 stalks of celery
1 large carrot
2 small onions, peeled
3 tbsp red pepper, chopped
2 eggs
300ml (½ pint) milk
Celery salt
Garlic salt
Freshly ground black pepper

Line a shallow pie dish with half the pastry. Finely chop the onions, carrot, celery and red peppers, and combine with the cheese. Beat eggs with milk and seasoning, and add to the vegetable mixture. Place all into pie case and cover with the remaining piece of pastry, reserving enough to decorate the top. Seal edges well. Slit top to allow steam to escape and decorate with pastry leaves. Brush with milk and bake in preheated oven 200C, 400F, Gas Mark 6 for 25–30 minutes until the pastry is well cooked and nicely browned. Serve with hot mixed vegetables or a side salad.

RHUBARB AND BANANA PIE

Serves 4

450g (1lb) rhubarb
75g (3oz) sugar
The grated rind of ½ a lemon
4 bananas
1 egg white
50g (2oz) almond flakes
2 tbsp caster sugar

Wash the rhubarb and cut into small lengths, put into a pie-dish and sprinkle with lemon rind and sugar. Peel the bananas, crush and beat to a pulp with the caster sugar; when soft beat in the white of the egg. Continue beating until quite stiff. Spread on the top of rhubarb to form a crust, sprinkle the top with blanched almonds, and bake in preheated oven 180C, 350F, Gas Mark 4 for about 30 minutes. Serve hot with custard or cream.

AUTUMN BLACKBERRY PUDDING

Serves 4–6

2 large eggs, beaten
110g (4oz) butter
110g (4oz) caster sugar
110g (4oz) self-raising flour
1 tsp baking powder
¼ tsp vanilla essence
175g (6oz) blackberries (picked
  over and cleaned)

Cream butter and sugar together. Add eggs, then flour, baking powder and vanilla essence, and beat well together. Place mixture in an ovenproof dish and top with blackberries, making sure there is plenty of room for the pudding to rise. Bake in preheated oven 190C, 375F, Gas Mark 5 for about 1 hour. Delicious served with ice-cream.

CHRISTMAS PUDDING (1)

This recipe is at least 150 years' old, and was given to me by a friend. It makes a dark, solid traditional pudding and keeps extremely well.

900g (2lb) raisins
900g (2lb) currants
450g (1lb) sultanas
450g (1lb) suet from butcher,
  chopped fine (I usually buy
  shredded suet from the
  supermarket)
225g (8oz) candied peel
450g (1lb) dark brown sugar
450g (1lb) plain flour
450g (1lb) breadcrumbs
1 sachet of spice
1 nutmeg, grated
6 eggs

Wine glass or so of brandy
600ml (1 pint) stout or beer

Clean fruit, mix well with all the other ingredients, taking care not to make it too wet. Put into greased basins, cover with greased paper and then a cloth. Boil for at least 6 to 8 hours. Dry well. Do not remove cloths or paper as the suet helps to seal for keeping. Steam or boil for another 4 to 5 hours on Christmas Day.

LIGHT CHRISTMAS PUDDING (2)

For those who may find pudding (1) a bit too heavy, this one is a much lighter version, and more easily digested.

450g (1lb) raisins
450g (1lb) fine breadcrumbs
225g (8oz) sultanas
4 tbsp milk
2 small wineglasses brandy
225g (8oz) mixed peel
450g (1lb) demerara sugar
8 eggs
350g (12oz) shredded suet
2 tsp mixed spice

Prepare fruit and mix all the dry ingredients together. Beat the yolks and white of eggs separately. Add them to the dry ingredients and then add the milk and brandy. Lightly grease basins and fill with the mixture, cover with grease-proof paper, then foil and steam for about 6–8 hours, and then steam for another 3 hours on Christmas Day.

MY QUICK CHRISTMAS PUDDING (3)

This pudding is for those who lead busy lives and just don't have time to make a Christmas Pudding in advance. It can be made on Christmas morning but, if you can, try to assemble the ingredients on Christmas Eve, and then hey presto! all you have to do is get one of the family to stir and mix the pudding for you!

50g (2oz) each of mixed peel,
    sultanas, currants and raisins
4 cherries, chopped
4 apricots, chopped
50g (2oz) mixed, chopped nuts
110g (4oz) butter
110g (4oz) demerara sugar
2 medium eggs, beaten
175g (6oz) self-raising flour
2 tsp mixed spice
1 tbsp brandy or rum

Beat butter and sugar until light and fluffy. Add beaten eggs, sifted flour and spice, and fold in gently. Add dried fruit and nuts, and brandy or rum, stirring to combine all the ingredients, add a little milk if necessary. Spoon into a greased 1.2 litre (2 pint) basin. Cover with greaseproof paper and foil, and tie round securely. Place in a saucepan filled with hot water halfway up the sides of the bowl, and simmer for 2–3 hours. Turn out and serve with brandy sauce or cream.

COFFEE FUDGE AND CREAM PUDDING

This pudding is for those with a sweet tooth and not counting calories!
Serves 6

225g (8oz) short crust pastry
75g (3oz) caster sugar
2 tbsp apricot jam
75g (3oz) butter
1 egg
35g (1½oz) chopped walnuts
110g (4oz) self-raising flour
2 dsp coffee essence
1 dsp cold milk
1 x 150g (5oz) carton soured cream

Roll out pastry and line a 20.5cm (8 inch) flan dish or tin with pastry. Spread base with apricot jam. Cream butter and sugar until light and fluffy, beat in eggs and walnuts, fold in flour alternately with coffee essence and milk, and put the mixture over the jam. Smooth the top with knife, and bake in the centre of preheated oven 220C, 425F, Gas Mark 7 for 15 minutes, then for a further 25–30 minutes at 170C, 325F, Gas Mark 3. Remove from oven, cover top with soured cream, and return to oven for a further 2 minutes.

MARMALADE PUDDING

Serves 4

2 eggs at room temperature
2 tbsp marmalade (not too chunky)
110g (4oz) unsalted butter
110g (4oz) caster sugar
110g (4oz) white breadcrumbs
1 tbsp self-raising flour
½ tsp bicarbonate of soda

Cut two rounds of greaseproof paper, one to fit the bottom of a pudding bowl and one for the top. Grease pudding bowl and paper circles. Place a tbsp of marmalade onto the paper at the base of the bowl. Beat butter and sugar until thick and light. Then beat eggs and add marmalade gradually to the beaten eggs. Fold in breadcrumbs, flour and bicarbonate. Place mixture into prepared pudding bowl. Cover with the larger circle of paper, and cover again with a large piece of tinfoil. Tie down firmly. Place in a large saucepan with boiling water to a depth of 1/3rd. Steam for approximately 3–4 hours, checking water level from time to time.

Delicious served with a hot whisky marmalade sauce made with 3 tbsp marmalade, 2 tbsp whisky and hot water to taste.

ORANGE MERINGUE BAKE

A quick and easy pudding to make when you are in a hurry.
Serves 4–6

600ml (1 pint) milk
Grated rind of 1 orange
1 tbsp sugar
25g (1oz) butter
75g (3oz) fine semolina
2 eggs
1 tbsp orange marmalade
2 extra tbsp caster sugar

Heat milk with grated orange rind, sugar and butter in saucepan.

Sprinkle in the semolina and bring to the boil, stirring. Remove from heat and beat in the egg yolks, marmalade and orange juice. Pour into greased fireproof dish. Whisk egg whites until stiff, gradually adding caster sugar, and pile on semolina mixture. Bake in preheated oven 190C, 375F, Gas Mark 5 for 25 minutes. Serve hot or chilled.

RHUBARB CRUMBLE

The combination of orange and rhubarb gives this crumble an added tangy flavour.
Serves 4

75g–110g (3–4oz) rolled oats
25g (1oz) plain flour
75g (3oz) butter
50g (2oz) soft brown sugar
Juice and zest of 1 small orange

Filling:
Approximately 450g (1lb)
    prepared rhubarb, 1 tbsp flour,
    3 tbsp soft brown sugar

Measure rolled oats, flour and baking powder into a bowl. Cut and rub in the butter. Add the soft brown sugar. The mixture should resemble breadcrumbs. Combine the prepared rhubarb with the flour and soft brown sugar, and arrange in a pie-dish. The dish should be approximately two thirds full. Sprinkle the crumb mixture over the top and bake in a preheated oven 180C, 350F, Gas Mark 4 for 40–45 minutes. Serve with cream or 'real' homemade custard.

PUDDINGS (COLD)

LEMON SYLLABUB TART

Serves 4–6

8 digestive biscuits
1 level tbsp caster sugar
35g (1½oz) butter

Filling:
1 small tin condensed milk, rind
    and juice of 1 large or 2 small
    lemons
4 tbsp double cream
110g (4oz) black grapes for
    decoration

Crush biscuits and add sugar. Melt butter, add biscuits and sugar. Stir until crumbs are quite buttery. Put mixture into 18cm (7") flan or pie plate. Using the back of a spoon, press mixture over base and around sides of the dish. Chill until firm. Mix condensed milk and cream. Stir in strained lemon juice and finely grated rind. Stir gently and mixture will thicken up in the bowl. Pour into prepared crumb crust and spread over level. Halve and deseed the black grapes and arrange around the rim of the tart. Chill before serving.

CHOCOLATE CHESTNUT CREAM

This pudding is definitely not for those on a slimming diet, but worth gaining the extra pounds!
Serves 4

245g (8¾oz) sweetened chestnut
    puree
110g (4oz) packet chocolate dots
1 egg yolk
2 tbsp brandy
10g (½oz) butter
10g (½oz) double cream
Chocolate buttons or curls for
    decoration

Melt chocolate with butter over hot, but not boiling, water. Remove and add beaten egg yolk. Beat in chestnut puree. Add brandy, whip cream and fold into chocolate. Reserve a little cream for decoration. Serve in individual glass dishes, and decorate when chilled.

RASPBERRY BRULEE

This pudding can be made the day before it is needed, and is quick and easy to prepare.
Serves 4

Put about 450g (1lb) of raspberries in an ovenproof dish. Cover generously with caster sugar and stand until sugar is dissolved. Whip 300ml (½pt) double cream until stiff and firm. Cover raspberries with this and then cover the cream with a layer of demerara sugar. Place under a very hot grill for one minute only, keeping watch all the time. Leave until cold and then refrigerate for at least two hours.

HONEYCOMB MOULD

Serves 4

3 eggs
600ml (1 pint) milk
75g (3oz) caster sugar
10g (½oz) powdered gelatine

Make custard by beating the separated egg yolks and sugar together, then adding the boiling milk and gelatine dissolved in 2 tbsp hot water. Allow to cool. Beat egg whites until stiff, and stir into custard, then pour into a wet ring mould. When set, turn out by inverting the mould over a plate. Use any fruit available for filling the centre of the mould. I use strawberries or raspberries when in season.

BANANA AND HONEY CHEESECAKE

Serves 6

Ingredients for the base:
225g (8oz) crushed wholewheat
    biscuits
75g (3oz) butter, melted

Filling:
110g (4oz) cream cheese, softened
300ml (½pt) whipping cream
25g (1oz) light muscovado sugar
2 tbsp clear honey
Juice and rind of half a lemon
2 medium bananas, mashed

Mix crushed biscuits and melted butter. Press into a greased 20.5cm (8 inch) flan dish. Chill. Beat together cream cheese, sugar, honey, lemon juice and rind. Fold in three quarters of the whipped cream and the mashed bananas. Spread over biscuit base. Decorate with cream and slices of crystallised lemon slices.

ORANGE FLUMMERY

Serves 4

300ml (½pt) water
25g (1oz) plain flour
20g (¾oz) butter
Grated rind and juice of 1 small
    orange
1 large egg
110g (4oz) caster sugar
Double cream to decorate

Put water, butter and grated rind into a pan and bring to the boil. Mix flour and sugar together in a bowl, make a well in the centre and pour in hot mixture, whisking well to avoid lumps, and return to pan. Put egg yolk into the bowl, whisk in a little of the hot liquid, then add to mixture in pan. Bring slowly to the boil, stirring all the time, and cook gently for 10 minutes. Add orange juice, then pour mixture into a bowl and fold in stiffly beaten egg white. Pour into a glass serving dish. Chill and decorate with cream.

LIME CUSTARD CREAM

Serves 4

1 lime jelly
150ml (¼pt) hot water
300ml (½pt) milk
2 eggs, separated

Place jelly in hot water and stir until dissolved. Heat milk to nearly boiling point. Beat egg yolks. Add a tbsp of milk to egg yolks, then gradually stir egg yolks into the remaining milk. Cook over a low heat, stirring constantly until thickened, but do not allow to boil. Stir the cooled, dissolved jelly into the custard. Whisk egg whites until fairly stiff and fold into mixture. Pour into a wet mould. Chill, and unmould when required. This jelly goes well with sliced peaches or apricots.

CHOCOLATE MOUSSE

Serves 4

Melt 110g (4oz) plain chocolate in a small bowl placed over a pan of hot water. Remove from the heat and stir in until smooth, 10g (½oz) butter, 3 egg yolks, a pinch of salt and 1 tsp brandy. Beat egg whites until stiff and fold into the chocolate mixture. Pour into four individual dishes and decorate with chopped nuts. Serve chilled.

PORT AND PRUNE FOOL

Serves 4

225g (8oz) Californian prunes (or a
   tin of prunes)
Lemon zest
175ml (6floz) Ruby Port
1 tbsp caster sugar
150ml (¼pt) double cream

Soak prunes in cold water for several hours. Poach them until tender in just sufficient water to cover with a good piece of lemon zest. Cool, remove the stones and if there is more than 3–4 tbsp of the cooking syrup, reduce it to that amount. Put the prunes, syrup and port in a liquidizer and blend until smooth. (There will be small flecks of skin.) Whip the cream, adding the sugar. When it is stiff, combine it with the prunes. Put the fool in tall stemmed glasses and chill. Serve with wafer biscuits.

APPLE ICE CREAM

Serves 4–6

300ml (½pt) apple puree
2 tsps lemon juice
Sugar to taste
300ml (½pt) cream
Pinch of ground nutmeg
Pinch of ground cinnamon

Mix apple puree, spices and lemon juice, and sweeten lightly. Chill for 1 hour. Fold in whipped cream and pour into freezing tray. Freeze until firm. Serve with butterscotch or raspberry sauce.

RHUBARB CHOCOLATE CAKE

This dessert cake has the refreshing taste of rhubarb coming through the chocolate. I always double up on the quantity and make one for the freezer, but it doesn't stay there long!

Serves 6

225g (8oz) rhubarb
75g (3oz) self-raising flour
10g (½oz) cocoa powder
Pinch of cinnamon
50g (2oz) soft brown or demerara
 sugar
35g (1½oz) butter, softened
1 egg
2–3 tbsp milk
10g (½oz) grated chocolate
10g (½oz) sifted icing sugar

Butter a 600ml (1pt) ovenproof dish or cake tin. Preheat oven to 180C, 350F, Gas Mark 4. Trim ends from rhubarb, wash and dry and cut into small pieces. Sift flour, cocoa and cinnamon into mixing bowl, add sugar, butter, egg and 2 tbsp of the milk. Beat until well mixed and smooth, adding more milk if necessary to make a fairly soft mixture. Stir in rhubarb and spread evenly in dish or cake tin. Bake in preheated oven for about 30 minutes. When cold dredge with chocolate powder, grated chocolate and icing sugar, and serve with clotted cream or ice cream. This pudding can also be served hot with custard

TOFFEE MOUSSE

This mousse is popular with children, who like the toffee flavour, but it's equally popular with grown-ups too!

Serves 4

4 eggs
10g (½oz) gelatine
300ml (½pt) cream, whipped
110g (4oz) black treacle

Separate eggs. Mix yolks and treacle. Melt gelatine in 150ml (¼pt) hot water, allow to cool. Whip cream and egg whites. Fold treacle mixture into cream, add cooled gelatine and then fold in stiffly beaten egg whites. Pour into glass serving dish or 4 individual dishes. Allow to set in refrigerator.

ELDERFLOWER SORBET

Serves 4–6

50g (2oz) elderflower heads
Juice and zest of 4 lemons
225g (8oz) caster sugar
850ml (1½pts) water
2 egg whites

Put sugar, lemon zest and water in a pan, and heat till sugar dissolves. Bring to the boil and simmer for 5 minutes. Add elderflower heads and lemon juice. Stir and cover. Leave to cool. Then strain and freeze for 2–3 hours until part frozen. Beat well, add whisked egg whites and refreeze.

CHOCOLATE BISCUIT CAKE

225g (8oz) plain chocolate
225g (8oz) butter or margarine
225g (8oz) rich tea biscuits
2 level dsp caster sugar
2 eggs
50g (2oz) chopped nuts
50g (2oz) glace cherries
Vanilla essence

Melt chocolate and butter or margarine in basin over hot water. Beat eggs and sugar thoroughly and add to mixture. Stir well. Add other ingredients, (biscuits should be broken). Pour mixture into a tin lined with greaseproof paper and leave to set. Decorate the top with coconut.

WALNUT CREAM FLAN

Make a sponge flan as follows:
Whisk together 3 small or 2 large eggs with 75g (3oz) caster sugar and finely grated rind of ½ a lemon until thick and creamy. Into this mixture fold in 35g (1½oz) melted butter and 75g (3oz) self-raising flour (fold in alternately, half at a time). Pour into a well greased flan tin and bake in preheated oven 180C, 350F, Gas Mark 4 for about 20–25 minutes.

When the flan is cold, fill with the following filling:
Cream together 110g (4oz) butter and 175g (6oz) caster sugar. Then beat two eggs into the mixture. Add 50g (2oz) finely chopped walnuts and a few drops of vanilla essence. Set aside for 24 hours, and then decorate with angelica and crystallised violets (optional). Serve with HOT chocolate sauce.

PINEAPPLE MERINGUE PIE

Serves 4–6

225g (8oz) wholewheat shortcrust
    pastry
2 level tbsp 81% wholewheat flour
110g (4oz) light muscovado sugar
Grated rind and juice 1 small
    lemon
150ml (¼pt) milk
2 tbsp cream
2 eggs separated
10g (½oz) butter
110g (4oz) fresh pineapple, finely
    chopped

Line 20.5cm (8 inch) flan dish with pastry. Bake blind in preheated oven 200C, 400F, Gas Mark 6 until crisp and golden. Mix flour, 50g (2oz) sugar, egg yolks, lemon rind and juice together in a basin until smooth. Heat milk and cream and carefully whisk in egg mixture. Stir continuously until it thickens. Beat in butter. Place pineapple in flan dish. Pour over custard. Allow to cool. Whisk egg whites until stiff, then fold in sugar, and pipe on top of flan. Bake in preheated oven 160C, 325F, Gas Mark 3 for approximately 30–40 minutes. Serve chilled.

RASPBERRY TRIFLE

I usually make this trifle at Christmas time, or for a party – it makes at least 8 generous servings.

6–8 individual stale sponge cakes
3 tbsp raspberry jam
150g (5oz) blanched almonds,
   separated into halves
150ml (¼pt) medium sherry
3 tbsp brandy
425ml (¾pt) double cream
2 tbsp caster sugar
350g (12oz) fresh raspberries, or
   equivalent frozen raspberries,
   defrosted and well drained
600ml (1pt) custard sauce

To make custard sauce: Heat 600ml (1pt) milk with vanilla pod, very gently in the top of a double saucepan (if you use vanilla essence instead of a pod, add it later with the sugar). Remove from heat and allow to infuse in a warm place for about half an hour. Then remove the pod. Beat 4 eggs lightly, but thoroughly. Add them to the barely warm milk in the double saucepan and reheat very gently, stirring frequently with a wooden spoon until the mixture becomes thick enough to coat the back of the spoon. Stir in 35g (1½oz) caster sugar and ½ tsp vanilla essence, if used. Strain and allow to get cold.

To assemble the trifle: Cut the sponge cakes into slices and coat them with the raspberry jam. Place 2 or 3 of the slices, jam side up, in the bottom of a large glass serving bowl. Cut the remaining sponge cakes into 2.5cm (1 inch) cubes, scatter them over the slices and sprinkle half the almonds on top. Then pour in the sherry and brandy and let the mixture steep at room temperature for at least 30 minutes. Whip the cream in a chilled bowl until it thickens slightly. Add the sugar and continue to beat until the cream is stiff. Set aside 10 of the best berries, and scatter the rest over the sponge cakes. Spread the custard across the top, smoothing with a spatula or large spoon. Then gently smooth half the whipped cream over the surface of the custard. Pipe the rest of the whipped cream around the edge of trifle. Garnish the cream with the 10 reserved berries and the rest of the almonds.

Trifle is always best served at once, but it may be refrigerated for an hour or two before it is needed.

Cakes and Traybakes

SMALL CAKES & TRAYBAKES

CHOCOLATE COCONUT BUNS

110g (4oz) butter
110g (4oz) caster sugar
2 eggs, beaten
110g (4oz) self-raising flour
110g (4oz) desiccated coconut
110g (4oz) chocolate cooking drops
2 tbsp milk

Cream the butter and sugar until light and fluffy. Add the beaten eggs, adding a little of the flour to prevent curdling. Fold in the remaining flour, coconut and chocolate drops, and then fold in the milk gently to soften the mixture. Divide between 18–20 greased patty tins and bake in preheated oven 180C, 350F, Gas Mark 4 for about 20–25 minutes until risen and golden brown. Turn out on wire tray to cool.

DATE AND CINNAMON CAKES

225g (8oz) self-raising flour
Pinch of salt
¼ tsp cinnamon
½ tsp baking powder
50g (2oz) butter
50g (2oz) caster sugar
110g (4oz) chopped dates
1 egg, beaten
300ml (½ pint) orange juice and
    water

Sieve the flour, salt, spices and baking powder together into a large mixing bowl. Add the butter and rub into mixture until it resembles breadcrumbs. Add sugar and chopped dates and mix to a firm dough with the egg and orange water. Place spoonfuls on a greased baking sheet and decorate each cake with a whole date. Bake in preheated oven 180C, 350F, Gas Mark 4 for 15–20 minutes.

CHOCOLATE BROWNIES

This recipe uses less sugar than is normally used for Chocolate Brownies, giving a more chocolaty flavour and crisper texture.

50g (2oz) walnuts
75g (3oz) butter
110g (4oz) plain flour
50g (2oz) caster sugar
50g (2oz) plain chocolate
1 medium egg
¼ tsp baking powder
¼ tsp salt
Milk to mix

Chop the walnuts and melt the chocolate in a basin over hot water. Cream together the butter and sugar and add well beaten egg. Sift in the flour, baking powder and salt and mix well. Now add the nuts, melted chocolate and just enough milk to bring mixture to a soft consistency. Spread the mixture into a greased baking or Swiss roll tin and dredge a little sugar on top. Bake in a preheated oven 180C, 350F, Gas Mark 4 for about 30 minutes. Cut into neat squares or fingers whilst still warm.

SPICY CAKES

175g (6oz) self-raising flour
75g (3oz) sultanas
75g (3oz) caster sugar
50g (2oz) treacle
50g (2oz) butter
1 egg, beaten
A little grated nutmeg
¾ tsp ground cinnamon

Mix all the dry ingredients together in a bowl. Melt treacle and butter in a small saucepan over a gentle heat, and then stir in beaten egg and add to the dry ingredients, mixing to a fairly soft batter. Divide into greased patty tins and bake in a hot oven preheated to 200C, 400F, Gas Mark 6 for 15–20 minutes. Cool on wire tray and sprinkle with icing sugar.

COCONUT CREAM CAKES

225g (8oz) self-raising flour
1 tsp baking powder
A pinch of salt
110g (4oz) butter
75g (3oz) caster sugar
60g (2½oz) coconut
1 egg, beaten
A little vanilla essence
Milk to mix

Sieve flour, baking powder and salt. Cut and rub in butter. Add the sugar, coconut, egg and vanilla essence, and mix all to a very stiff dough, adding a little milk if necessary. Put in small rough heaps on a greased baking tray and bake in preheated oven 230C, 450F, Gas Mark 8 for 15 minutes.

Filling:
40g (1½oz) butter
65g (2½oz) icing sugar
Vanilla essence
Few drops of cochineal

Cream the butter, and gradually beat in the sieved icing sugar. Flavour with vanilla essence and colour delicately with the cochineal. When the cakes are cold split diagonally and sandwich together with the filling, and dust with icing sugar.

LITTLE SURPRISE CAKES

These dainty little cakes live up to their name, and you can vary the flavour of your filling according to your taste.

110g (4oz) self-raising flour
75g (3oz) butter or margarine
75g (3oz) caster sugar
2 tbsp milk
1 egg
¼ tsp ground nutmeg
1 tsp vanilla essence

Cream butter and sugar and beat in the egg. Add the flour sifted with nutmeg, and lastly milk and vanilla essence. Bake in deep well-greased patty tins in a hot oven preheated to 200C, 400F, Gas Mark 6 for about 15 minutes or until golden brown and well risen. When completely cold scoop out the centre of each cake and fill with some thick vanilla or chocolate custard, or whipped cream, lemon curd or jam. Carefully replace the thin layer on top and ice as though nothing had happened!

COFFEE NUT CAKES

50g (2oz) butter
50g (2oz) caster sugar
75g (3oz) self-raising flour
1 egg
2 tbsp milk
1 dsp coffee essence
25g (1oz) finely chopped walnuts

Beat butter and sugar until fluffy and creamy. Beat the egg with the milk, and add it to the creamed mixture. Beat thoroughly with a little flour. Fold in the rest of the flour. Stir in the coffee essence and walnuts and turn into a dozen greased patty tins. Bake in a fairly hot oven (preheated to 200C, 400F, Gas Mark 6) for about 10–15 minutes. When cakes are cool, cover tops with coffee icing and place a piece of walnut on each one.

SNOWBALLS

These cakes are great for children's parties.

75g (3oz) butter or margarine
75g (3oz) caster sugar
120g (4½oz) self-raising flour
1 egg
1 tbsp milk
½ tsp vanilla

Cream butter and sugar together, add beaten egg and vanilla essence and beat well. Stir in the milk, then add the sifted flour. Beat for one minute and spoon into greased patty tins or paper cases. Bake in preheated oven 200C, 400F, Gas Mark 6 for about 10–15 minutes. When cold dip in a very thin chocolate icing and roll immediately in coarse coconut. Make some vanilla flavoured mock cream (if you have fresh cream, it is of course, better), make a slit in the side of each cake near the top and fill it with the cream.

LITTLE SCOTCH BUNS

110g (4oz) rich short crust pastry
110g (4oz) caster sugar
110g (4oz) butter
150g (5oz) plain flour
1 dsp treacle
½ tsp bicarbonate of soda
2 eggs
350g (12oz) mixed dried fruit
50g (2oz) chopped peel
¼ tsp each cinnamon, nutmeg and
    spice
12 blanched almonds
1 tbsp brandy or sherry

Prepare the fruit, sprinkle the brandy or sherry on top and cover tightly. Roll out the pastry and grease small deep patty tins. Cream the butter, sugar and spices, and beat in the eggs separately and thoroughly, then add the treacle. Sift the flour with the bicarbonate, and add alternately with the fruit. Spoon the mixture into the greased tins and top each cake with a blanched almond. Put into a preheated oven 180C, 350F, Gas Mark 4 and bake fairly slowly until the cakes and pastry are both cooked.

PEANUT BISCUITS

These biscuits are easy to make, and the dough can be frozen if you want to make a small quantity.
Makes about 18–20

110g (4oz) butter or margarine
75g (3oz) soft brown sugar
75g (3oz) caster sugar
1 medium egg, beaten
75g (3oz) crunchy peanut butter
175g (6oz) plain flour
½ tsp baking powder
Pinch of salt

Cream butter and sugar together until smooth. Beat in the egg and the peanut butter. Sift the flour and salt and baking powder into the mixture and beat lightly until smooth. Roll the mixture into balls the size of a walnut and place well apart on a greased baking sheet, and flatten with the prongs of a fork that has been dipped in water, to stop sticking. Bake in preheated oven 180C, 350F, Gas Mark 4 for 12–15 minutes until lightly golden. Cool on baking tray and store in an airtight container.

GINGER CAKE TRAYBAKE

350g (12oz) self-raising flour
1 level tsp bicarbonate of soda
3 rounded tsps ground ginger
200g (7oz) caster sugar
110g (4oz) soft margarine
1 large egg
2 tbsp golden syrup
225ml (8floz) boiling milk, plus a
    little extra if needed

Preheat oven to 150C, 300F, Gas Mark 2. Grease and line a Swiss roll tin about 28cm x 18cm (11 inches x 7 inches). Sieve flour and soda into a bowl, add all the other ingredients and mix thoroughly until the mixture is soft and smooth. Pour into prepared tin, and bake for about 45 minutes, until the cake is firm and slightly shrunk from the sides of the tin. Turn out onto a wire tray to allow cooling, then cut into squares.

RASPBERRY ICED TRAYBAKE

175g (6oz) self-raising flour
1 raspberry flavoured blancmange
    powder
150g (5oz) soft margarine
150g (5oz) caster sugar
2 tbsp raspberry jam
2 eggs
A little milk

Grease and line a 30.5cm x 23cm (12 inch x 9 inch) tray bake tin. Sieve flour together with blanc-mange powder. Cream together the margarine, sugar and jam, and gradually beat the eggs into this mixture. Stir in the flour and add a few drops of milk to give a creamy consistency. Put into the lined tin and bake for approximately 25–30 mins. in preheated oven 180C, 350F, Gas Mark 4. When completely cold ice with glacé icing coloured with a little cochineal, or you can beat one egg white until very stiff, and gradually whisk in 1 tbsp of hot raspberry jam and spread over the top of the cake. Cut into fingers or squares.

LEMON SQUARES

Juice and zest of 1 large lemon
75g (3oz) butter, melted
110g (4oz) caster sugar
3 eggs
75g (3oz) self-raising flour
110g (4oz) ground almonds
75g (3oz) icing sugar
Juice of half a lemon

Put the large lemon into a pan and cover with cold water. Bring to the boil, then cover with a lid, reduce the heat and simmer for about 35 minutes. Remove from pan and transfer to a plate to cool completely. Preheat oven to 180C, 350F, Gas Mark 4. Grease and line a Swiss roll tin 28cm x 18cm (11 inches x 7 inches). Cut the lemon into 4 quarters and remove and discard pips, then tip into food processor and whiz until smooth. Put the sugar and eggs in a large bowl and whisk with an electric hand whisk until light and fluffy, about 10 minutes. Sift the flour and ground almonds into the mixing bowl, mix with a metal spoon until the flour and ground almonds have become combined. Add the lemon puree and melted butter, and fold in gently until just mixed. Pour mixture into prepared tin and bake for about 35–40 minutes until the cake is lightly brown on top. Cool completely on wire rack, then make a smooth icing with the icing sugar and the juice of half a lemon, and drizzle over the cake. Cut into squares or fingers.

RAISIN FINGERS

150g (5oz) soft margarine
150g (5oz) caster sugar
3 eggs
50g (2oz) plain chocolate drops
175g (6oz) self-raising flour
75g (3oz) seedless raisins
A little icing sugar

Line a Swiss roll tin with greased paper. Cream margarine and sugar until soft and light. Gradually beat in eggs, stir in sieved flour, and add chocolate drops and raisins to the mixture. Spread in tin and bake for approximately 25 minutes in preheated oven 180C, 350F, Gas Mark 4. Cool and cover the top with sieved icing sugar. Cut into fingers.

OATY APRICOT MUFFINS

115g (4½oz) plain flour
50g (2oz) wheat germ
50g (2oz) rolled oats
110g (4oz) soft brown sugar
1 tsp baking powder
1 tsp bicarbonate of soda
110g (4oz) apricots, chopped
100ml (4floz) buttermilk
2 tbsp sunflower oil
2 egg whites, lightly beaten

Preheat oven to 200C, 400F, Gas Mark 6. Set 8 large muffin cases into a muffin tin. Combine all the dry ingredients in a large bowl. In a separate bowl, combine the remaining ingredients. Put the wet ingredients into the dry and mix until moist, but still lumpy. Spoon the mixture into cases and bake for 18–20 minutes until golden. Serve warm or cold.

PINEAPPLE MINCEMEAT SQUARES

450g (1lb) plain flour
Pinch of salt
110g (4oz) butter or margarine
110g (4oz) lard
4–5 tbsp cold water to mix
Milk to glaze
Caster sugar for sprinkling

Pineapple filling:
450g (16oz) can pineapple pieces
350g (¾lb) mincemeat

To prepare filling: Drain and chop the pineapple and mix into the mincemeat.

Sift the flour and salt in a bowl and rub in the fats lightly until the mixture resembles fine bread-crumbs. Mix to a firm dough with the cold water. Turn on to a lightly floured board, knead until smooth. Roll out two-thirds of the pastry and use to line an oblong tin approximately 30.5cm x 20.5cm (12 inches x 8 inches), spread with the prepared filling. Damp edges of pastry with water. Roll remaining pastry out into an oblong for the lid. Lift on to the filling, seal firmly, trim and pinch up edges into a neat border. Brush with milk. Place in a preheated oven 200C, 400F, Gas Mark 6 for 30–35 minutes until golden brown. Allow to cool in the tin. Sprinkle with a little caster sugar. Makes about 12.

TRAYBAKE ROCK CAKES

225g (8oz) self-raising flour
110g (4oz) soft margarine
50g (2oz) caster sugar
1 egg
110g (4oz) dried fruit
1 tbsp milk
25g (1oz) demerara sugar

Rub margarine into flour, stir in sugar and fruit. Add beaten egg and milk to mix. Spoon into a fairly large Swiss roll tin and even out the top with a knife. Sprinkle with demerara sugar and bake in preheated oven 200C, 400F, Gas Mark 6 for 25 minutes. Cool on wire tray and then cut into fingers.

CHOCOLATE AND LIME SQUARES

3 tbsp cocoa
3 tbsp boiling water
175g (6oz) soft margarine
175g (6oz) caster sugar
3 eggs
225g (8oz) self-raising flour
1½ tsp baking powder
3 tbsp lime marmalade

Icing:
75g (3oz) block margarine
50g (2oz) cocoa
225g (8oz) icing sugar
2 tbsp milk

Blend cocoa with the boiling water and leave to cool, and then add margarine, sugar and eggs. Sift flour and baking powder over mixture and beat until smooth. Place in a lined fairly deep 30.5cm x 20.5cm (12" x 8") tin and bake at 180C, 350F, Gas Mark 4 for about 40 minutes. Warm marmalade and spread over. Melt margarine and stir in sifted cocoa and sifted icing sugar. Beat in the milk and heat gently. Spoon icing over the cake and cut into squares.

FRUIT AND NUT SHORTBREAD

225g (8oz) plain flour
25g (1oz) ground rice
175g (6oz) butter
75g (3oz) caster sugar
25g (1oz) glace cherries, chopped
25g (1oz) angelica, chopped
35g (1½oz) flaked almonds

Cream butter and sugar, add prepared nuts and fruit, and mix in the flour and ground rice sifted together. Form the mixture into a smooth ball and roll it out for a square shape. Cut a square a little smaller than your tin, and put the shortbread into a greased and lined 18cm (7 inch) square tin, and lightly press a few almond flakes on top of the mixture. Bake shortbread in preheated oven 180C, 350F, Gas Mark 4 for about 30 minutes until it is crisp and golden. Cut into squares or fingers, and sprinkle with a little caster sugar.

MACAROON MINCE PIES

Makes 12

175g (6oz) plain white flour
Pinch of salt
75g (3oz) butter
225g (8oz) homemade (or good
    quality) mincemeat
2 egg whites
75 (3oz) caster sugar
110g (4oz) ground almonds
1 small egg yolk
Icing sugar

Sieve together the flour and salt. Rub in butter until mixture resembles fine breadcrumbs. Stir in egg yolk and 2–3 tbsp water and knead lightly to form a smooth dough. Wrap in cling film and chill for about 15 minutes. Roll out pastry on lightly floured surface, stamp out 12 rounds with a 8cm (3 inch) fluted pastry cutter and grease 6cm (2½ inch) patty tins. Bake blind for 12–15 minutes at 180C, 350F, Mark 4 until set and lightly browned. Cool in tin and fill pastry cases with mincemeat. Whisk egg whites until stiff, but not too dry. Whisk in caster sugar, keeping mixture stiff, fold in ground almonds. Divide mixture among pastry cases, spreading out to cover mincemeat completely. Bake at 180C, 350F, Gas Mark 4 for about 20 minutes until lightly golden. Cool, and serve hot or cold, dusted with icing sugar. These pies will freeze well.

APPLE TURNOVERS

Peel, core and finely chop 6 tart apples. Melt 4 tbsp butter in saucepan and sauté apples for about 6 minutes, until partially cooked. Remove from heat and add sugar to taste. Add tbsp rum or brandy and a tsp vanilla essence, and set aside to cool.

Meanwhile roll out 4 to 6 rounds of puff pastry (I use a medium sized dessert plate as a guide), moisten edges and fill the centres with the apple mixture. Fold circle of pastry in half to enclose filling and crimp up edges to form a border. Brush with beaten egg and sprinkle with demerara sugar. Bake in preheated oven 230C, 450F, Gas Mark 8 for 25–30 minutes until golden brown. Serve warm as a dessert or make smaller ones and serve cooled for tea.

CHOCOLATE ÉCLAIRS

Éclairs can be a bit tricky to make, but once you've mastered the choux pastry the rest is easy, and you will enjoy eating homemade ones too!

Choux pastry:
110g (4oz) plain flour
300ml (½ pint) water
Pinch of salt
50g (2oz) butter
½ tsp vanilla essence
1 egg yolk and 2 eggs

Sift and warm the flour. Place water, salt and fat in a saucepan and bring to the boil. Remove from heat, add flour all at once and beat well with a wooden spoon over the heat until it is a smooth soft paste and leaves the sides of the saucepan clean. Remove from heat, add vanilla essence and egg yolk and beat well. Add the other two eggs one at a time, beating well between each addition, this should be done as quickly as possible while the mixture is still warm. Use as required.

Place a sufficient quantity of pastry in a forcing bag with a 1" nozzle and pipe mixture out on to a greased baking sheet in 10cm (4 inch) lengths, cutting off each length with a knife, which has been dipped into hot water. Bake in preheated oven 220C, 425F, Gas Mark 7 until risen and crisp. Reduce heat a little and leave éclairs to cook further until they are light and dry inside. Usually about 25–30 minutes altogether. Place on a cooling tray and slit open. When cold fill the cavities with whipped cream flavoured with vanilla essence and spread tops with dark chocolate glace icing.

LARGE CAKES & SPECIAL OCCASION CAKES

∽

ORANGE SPONGE CAKE

175g (6oz) soft margarine
175g (6oz) caster sugar
3 large eggs
175g (6oz) self-raising flour
1½ level tsp baking powder
  (sieved together)
Grated rind of 1 orange

Place all the ingredients into a mixing bowl and beat with an electric mixer or a wooden spoon until smooth. Divide between two 18cm (7 inch) sponge tins, greased and bottom-lined. Smooth tops. Bake on middle shelf of preheated oven 170C, 325F, Gas Mark 3 for 25–30 minutes. Turn out and cool on wire tray.

Icing:
50g (2oz) soft margarine
4 tbsp orange juice or milk
275g (10oz) icing sugar

Place ingredients in a bowl over hot water and mix until smooth. Use 2/3rd icing as a filling for two halves of cake and ice top of cake with remainder.

WALNUT COFFEE CAKE

50g (2oz) walnut pieces
110g (4oz) soft margarine
110g (4oz) caster sugar
2 standard eggs
75g (3oz) self-raising flour
1 level tsp baking powder
25g (1oz) porridge oats

Icing:
35g(1½oz) butter
1 tbsp milk
2–3 rounded tsp instant coffee
Hot water
225g (8oz) icing sugar
Walnut halves to decorate

Grease and line 20cm (8 inch) sandwich tin with greaseproof paper greased. Chop walnuts finely. Beat margarine, sugar, eggs, flour and baking powder with wooden spoon or electric mixer for approx. 1–2 minutes until thoroughly blended. Fold in oats and walnuts. Spread mixture in tin and level top. Bake in centre of preheated oven 180C, 350F, Gas Mark 4 for approximately 40 mins. Leave in tin for 5–10 minutes. Turn out and cool on wire tray.

To make icing: Put 35g (1½oz) butter and milk in a pan and stir over low heat to melt. Remove from heat. Dissolve coffee in 1 tbsp hot water. Add to pan with icing sugar – heat until thick. Coat top and sides of cake with icing and decorate with walnut halves.

FRUIT CAKE

A quickly made fruitcake. Makes one 2lb cake or two 1lb cakes.

175g (6oz) soft margarine
175g (6oz) soft brown sugar
3 eggs
225g (8oz) self-raising flour
50g (2oz) quartered glace cherries
350g (12oz) mixed dried fruit
3 level tbsp marmalade
2 tbsp milk

Mix all ingredients together until well blended and place in two 450g (1lb) loaf tins lined with grease-proof paper. Level the tops and bake at 170C, 325F, Gas Mark 3 for 1¾ hours. Cool in tin for 10 minutes, then cool on wire rack.

WALNUT AND DATE CAKE

This cake freezes well, with or without icing, and the lemon and honey topping gives it a nice tangy taste.

225g (8oz) stoned and chopped dates
110g (4oz) soft brown sugar
110g (4oz) hard margarine
300ml (½ pint) water
2 eggs, lightly beaten
110g (4oz) walnuts, chopped
250g (9oz) self-raising flour (I use half wholemeal and half white, but either will do)

Icing:
50g (2oz) icing sugar
2 tsp runny honey
4 tsp lemon juice and a little water

Place the dates, brown sugar, margarine and water in a saucepan and melt, but do not boil. When cool, add the melted mixture to the sifted flour, and add the walnuts. Add the eggs and mix well. Turn into a lined and greased 1kg (2lb) loaf tin and bake in preheated oven 170C, 325F, Gas Mark 3 for 1–1¼ hours. Cool in tin and, when cold, pour over the icing, which has been mixed thoroughly.

APRICOT WHOLEMEAL CAKE

A wholesome standby cake, good for lunch boxes, and freezes well.

350g (12oz) dried apricots, chopped
110g (4oz) butter
110g (4oz) soft brown sugar
1 tbsp honey
300ml (½ pint) water
1 tsp ground cinnamon and nutmeg
2 eggs, lightly beaten
250g (9oz) self-raising wholemeal flour
2 tsp baking powder

Melt the first six ingredients in a saucepan gently. Pour into a mixing bowl and add flour and baking powder. Mix well, cool slightly, and add lightly beaten eggs. Mix well again. Turn the mixture into the prepared tin and bake on the middle shelf of pre-heated oven 190C, 375F, Gas Mark 5 for 45–50 minutes. Test with a skewer to make sure cake is cooked through. Cool in tin.

THREE-TIER CHOCOLATE CAKE

This is a moist cake, and keeps well; can also be used as a pudding with cream, if you aren't counting calories!

175g (6oz) self-raising flour
175g (6oz) caster sugar
175g (6oz) butter
2 eggs
50g (2oz) cocoa
6 tbsp warm water
2 tsp baking powder

For the filling:
225g (8oz) butter, softened
50g (2oz) cocoa
275g (10oz) icing sugar

To make filling: Cream softened butter and sifted icing sugar. Add sifted cocoa powder to mixture and beat thoroughly. Set aside until needed.

Put all the cake ingredients into a mixing bowl, and beat until light and fluffy. Put into three sandwich tins and cook in preheated oven 180C, 350F, Gas Mark 4 for about 25–30 minutes. Sandwich together with chocolate filling.

LEMON CARAWAY CAKE

225g (8oz) self-raising flour
Pinch of salt
175g (6oz) butter
110g (4oz) caster sugar
5 tbsp lemon curd
3 standard eggs
1 level tsp caraway seeds
   (optional)

Sieve flour and salt. Cream the butter and caster sugar together in the lemon curd and beat in the eggs one at a time. Stir in the caraway seeds and lightly fold in the flour. Turn the mixture into a greased and lined 18cm (7 inch) cake tin and bake in the centre of a preheated oven 170C, 325F, Gas Mark 3 for about one hour. Let the cake cool for 10 minutes before turning out onto a wire tray. Made with homemade lemon curd, this cake is delicious, and disappears quickly!

AMERICAN SNOW CAKE

Children love this cake, and it's ideal for a birthday party.

150g (5oz) self-raising flour
75g (3oz) butter
75g (3oz) caster sugar
1 egg and the yolk of one egg

Cream the butter and sugar together. Add well beaten egg and egg yolk, and lastly add the sieved flour. Turn into an 18cm (7 inch) cake tin and bake in preheated oven 180C, 350F, Gas Mark 4 for about 40 minutes. When cooked and cooled on wire tray, cut cake in two horizontally and fill and ice cake as follows:

Filling: 75g (3oz) butter beaten with ½ teacup of icing sugar. Stir in ½ teacup of coconut.

Icing: Beat stiffly the white of the extra egg yolk, and when stiff add ½ teacup of icing sugar, and lastly ½ teacup of coconut.

CHERRY FRUIT CAKE

175g (6oz) plain flour
110g (4oz) butter
110g (4oz) caster sugar
2 eggs
110g (4oz) glace cherries, cut into
    quarters
2 tsp baking powder

Cream butter and sugar, and add well-beaten eggs. Sieve the flour and baking powder and fold into the creamed mixture. Lastly add the quartered cherries. Put into a greased and lined 18cm (8 inch) cake tin and bake in preheated oven 170–180C, 325–350F, Gas Mark 3–4 for approximately 1½ hours until the cake is cooked through. Cool on wire tray.

APPLE CAKE

350g (12oz) self-raising flour
225g (8oz) butter
175g (6oz) soft brown sugar
450g (1lb) diced apples
110g (4oz) sultanas
3 large eggs

Topping:
2 tbsp demerara sugar
1 tsp ground cloves

Rub butter into flour and beat in eggs one at a time. Fold in fruit and apples. Turn into a well-greased 20.5cm (8 inch) cake tin and sprinkle the top of the cake with the sugar and cloves. Bake in the centre of a preheated oven 180C, 350F, Gas Mark 4 for approximately 1–1¼ hours. To serve cut into slices spread with a little butter, or serve as a pudding with whipped cream.

CIDER CAKE

225g (8oz) self-raising flour
110g (4oz) caster sugar
110g (4oz) butter
2 eggs
1 tsp bicarbonate of soda
¼ nutmeg, well grated
1 teacupful cider (not too sweet)

Beat the butter and sugar to a cream. Add the eggs, well beaten, then 110g (4oz) of the flour sifted with the bicarbonate of soda and the nutmeg. Pour over all the cider beaten to a froth and mix thoroughly. Stir in the remaining 110g (4oz) of flour and mix well together. Bake in a shallow well greased and lined tin (I use a square 8 inch cake tin) in preheated oven 180C, 350F, Gas Mark 4 for about 45 minutes. This cake is delicious with a tangy distinctive flavour.

SWISS ROLL

75g (3oz) plain flour
1 level tsp baking powder
110g (4oz) caster sugar
Pinch of salt
3 eggs
1 tbsp hot water
A little caster sugar for dredging
3–4 tbsp warm jam or lemon curd

Grease and line a 23cm x 30.5cm (9in x 12in) Swiss roll tin. Sift flour, baking powder and salt into a small basin. Place eggs and sugar in a bowl over a pan of gently steaming hot water, and whisk together until very thick and creamy. Remove bowl from water and continue whisking until mixture is cool. Fold in flour mixture as lightly as possible with a metal spoon, and lastly fold in hot water.

Pour into the prepared tin and spread out evenly with a gentle tap on table. Bake in preheated oven at 200C, 400F, Gas Mark 6 for 8–10 minutes until pale golden and springy (do not overcook). Turn out the sponge on to a piece of grease-proof paper well sprinkled with caster sugar and strip off the lining paper. Trim off crisp edges with a sharp knife, and spread almost to the edge with 4 tbsp of warm jam. Then lift the edges of the sugared paper nearest to you and roll the sponge into a neat and firm roll, then stand roll join side down on a cooling rack. When completely cold sprinkle with more caster sugar before serving. This Swiss roll is best eaten at once, but it can be stored overnight in an airtight tin.

PEACH CREAM ANGEL CAKE

This cake is ideal for a special celebration, or a Mother's Day Cake.

75g (3oz) plain flour
10g (½oz) cornflour
175g (6oz) caster sugar
6 large egg whites
1 tsp cream of tartar
1 tsp vanilla essence
300ml (½ pint) whipping cream
50g (2oz) vanilla flavoured sugar
Angelica
Peach brandy

Preheat oven to 170C, 325F, Gas Mark 3. Sieve flour with cornflour and 110g (4oz) of the sugar onto greaseproof paper. Whisk egg whites with cream of tartar in a wide bowl until stiff and fluffy, but still a bit moist. Sprinkle remaining sugar over egg whites and gently whisk in, and fold in vanilla essence. Sieve flour mixture into

bowl, folding it in at the same time. Spoon mixture into an ungreased, non-stick 25cm (10 inch) ring tin, smooth, level and bake for 45–55 minutes. Cool in tin for 10 minutes, then loosen and turn onto a wire rack to cool.

To make peach cream, beat cream with sugar until thick and smooth. Flavour to taste with peach brandy and, if desired, tint pale green or yellow with 1–2 drops of food colouring. Spread over cake and decorate with chopped angelica. For a profes-sional touch, decorate with fresh violets and primroses. Brush flowers lightly with whisked egg white, dust with caster sugar and put on non-stick paper. Leave in a warm place to dry.

VICTORIA SPONGE SANDWICH

Always a favourite for tea-time, can be made in one stage and you can vary fillings to your taste, but I think jam and cream is one of the nicest.

175g (6oz) self-raising flour
Pinch of salt
175g (6oz) soft margarine
175g (6oz) caster sugar
3 large eggs, beaten
1–2 tbsp milk

2–3 tbsp of jam or butter icing, a
   little caster or icing sugar

Sift flour and salt together and set aside. Cream margarine and sugar together thoroughly. Lightly beat eggs into creamed mixture a little at a time, beating between additions. Using a metal spoon, lightly fold in flour, adding only sufficient milk to make a soft dropping consistency. Divide the mixture between two 20cm (8 inch) sandwich tins, lightly greased and base lined with a circle of greased greaseproof paper. Spread the mixture evenly, slightly hollowing out the centre. Place in centre of preheated oven 190C, 375F, Gas Mark 5 and bake for about 20 minutes, or until risen and brown, and slightly shrunk from the sides of the tins. To test if cooked, press the centre of each sponge cake with the finger. If the surface is firm and the finger mark disappears, the sandwich is baked. Remove sandwich from oven and leave in the tins for 2–3 minutes. Then turn out, remove paper and leave to cool on a wire tray. When cold, sandwich the two cakes with a layer of jam or butter icing, or both. Sprinkle the top with caster or icing sugar.

WHISKED FATLESS SPONGE

Another teatime treat, which is easy, and can be whipped up in a matter of minutes.

110g (4oz) self-raising flour
2 large eggs
110g (4oz) caster sugar
1 tbsp warm water
2–3 tbsp of jam or mock cream

Mock Cream:
50g (2oz) caster sugar
50g (2oz) butter
6 tsp of very hot water
4 tsp of cold milk
Few drops of vanilla essence

Cream butter with sugar until light and fluffy. Gradually beat in very hot water, then cold milk. Add vanilla essence and beat until light. Use as required.

Sift flour twice and put aside in a warm place. Break eggs into a large bowl and then add caster sugar. Place bowl containing eggs and the sugar over a pan of hot water and whisk until the mixture is very thick and light in colour. Remove from water and continue whisking until mixture is quite cool. Then stir in warm water. Using a metal spoon, lightly fold in flour using as few strokes as possible. Divide sponge mixture between two 15cm (6 inch) tins that have been greased and lined with greased paper on the bottoms. Place in the centre of a preheated oven 200C, 400F, Gas Mark 6 and bake for 15 minutes, or until risen and brown. When cooked turn onto a wire tray and leave to cool. Sandwich with jam or mock cream, and dust top of sponge with icing sugar.

CHRISTMAS CAKE

350g (12oz) currants
350g (12oz) sultanas
350g (12oz) seedless raisins
75g (3oz) cherries, chopped
150g (5oz) chopped apricots
75g (3oz) chopped dates
110g (4oz) chopped almonds
110g (4oz) finely chopped candied
  peel
450g (1lb) plain flour
1 level tsp salt
1 level tsp allspice
1 level tsp nutmeg
350g (12oz) butter
350g (12oz) dark brown sugar
Finely grated rind of 1 lemon
6 medium eggs
1 tbsp golden syrup
1 tbsp black treacle
3 tbsp brandy or sherry

Grease a 22cm (9 inch) cake tin lined with a double layer of greased greaseproof paper. Sift flour with salt and spices. Cream softened butter with sugar and finely grated lemon rind until light and fluffy. Add the eggs, one at a time, beating well after each addition. Fold in sifted flour mixture with all the fruits and nuts, golden syrup and black treacle, brandy or sherry. Turn the mixture into prepared cake tin and bake on shelf below centre of a very slow oven 140C, 275F, Gas Mark 1 for approximately 5–6 hours, or until cooked completely through. Cover with a piece of greaseproof paper after about 2½ hours cooking time. Test cake before you take it out of the oven. Cool cake in tin then turn out on to a cooling rack, remove paper and when cold store in airtight tin.

To almond paste I recommend buying the commercially made, which I find excellent. You will need enough to almond paste a 22cm (9 inch) cake.

Before almond pasting cake, brush the top of cake (and sides if you are going to paste all over) with warmed apricot glaze.

Royal Icing:
700g (1½lb) sifted icing sugar
3 large egg whites
1 dessertspoon of strained lemon
  juice

Place the egg whites and strained lemon juice in a bowl and beat to a froth with a wooden spoon. Add the icing sugar, a heaped table-spoonful at a time, beating well after each addition. Continue adding the icing sugar until the icing stands in firm peaks. Set aside and keep covered with a damp cloth to prevent a crust forming. This amount of icing will cover the top and sides of the cake. Use a palette knife dipped in hot water to ease spreading the icing over the cake.

Scones and
Biscuits

MY VERY LIGHT SCONES

I have been using this recipe for more years than I care to remember, and it produces feather-light scones every time. You can, if you wish, omit the sugar and fruit, and when cooked just spread the scones with cream and jam.

225g (8oz) plain flour
1 dsp baking powder
½ tsp salt
50g (2oz) butter
25g (1oz) caster sugar
25g (1oz) sultanas
10g (½oz) candied lemon peel
Milk to mix

Sieve flour, baking powder and salt, and rub in the butter. Add sugar, sultanas and peel, and mix altogether with milk to form a soft dough. Knead lightly and turn out onto a floured board, and roll or pat out to about 2.5cm (1 inch) thick. Then cut into rounds with 5cm (2 inch) cutter. Brush with beaten egg or milk and bake in preheated oven 230C, 450F, Gas Mark 8 for about 15 minutes.

HONEY SCONE ROUNDS

450g (1lb) Granary Bread Flour
2 level tsp bicarbonate of soda
1 level tsp cream of tartar
½ level tsp salt
75g (3oz) margarine
50g (2oz) soft brown sugar
2 level tbsp honey
300ml (½ pint) milk

Put Granary Bread Flour into a mixing bowl, then sift the bircarbonate of soda, cream of tartar and the salt into it. Rub the margarine into the mixture then stir in the sugar. Mix the honey into the milk, keeping back 1 tbsp for the glaze. Mix the ingredients into a soft dough, then turn this onto a floured surface. Cut the dough in half and lightly knead each piece into a round about 15cm (6 inches) in diameter, and place these on floured baking trays. Mark each into 6 wedges with a knife and brush the tops with the rest of the milk and honey. Bake scones in preheated oven 200C, 400F, Gas Mark 6 for about 20 minutes. Cool the scones between the folds of a tea towel to keep the tops soft. Eat warm with butter and honey – delicious!

DROP SCONES

225g (1lb) plain flour
1 tsp baking powder
300ml (½pt) milk
75g (3oz) caster sugar
2 eggs, beaten
Pinch of salt

Sift all the dry ingredients together in a large mixing bowl. Add the eggs, and gradually add the milk until the mixture is of a creamy consistency. Heat a girdle pan, grease with butter and lightly flour. Drop tbsps of the mixture onto the hot girdle, and when bubbles appear on the surface turn the drop scones over and cook on the other side. Cool between two cloths, or you can serve them hot with butter and raspberry jam.

CHEESE SCONES

These scones can be made in one stage and make a quick tea-time favourite.

50g (2oz) luxury margarine (Blue Band)
225g (8oz) self-raising flour
1 rounded tsp baking powder
¼ level tsp salt, ½ level tsp dry mustard, sieved together
75g (3oz) Cheddar cheese, finely grated
5 tbsp milk
1 small egg
Milk to glaze

Put all the ingredients into a mixing bowl. Mix thoroughly to form a scone dough. Turn onto a lightly floured surface. Roll out to 1cm (½ inch) thickness. Cut into rounds with a 5cm (2 inch) cutter. Brush the tops with milk. Put onto a baking sheet and bake for 12–15 minutes. 220C, 425F, Gas Mark 7.

FRUITY SCONES

Makes two rounds, which can be cut into six portions each.

2 tea cups plain flour
½ tsp bicarbonate of soda
½ tsp cream of tartar
Pinch of salt
2 medium eggs, well beaten
Butter the weight of one egg
2 dsp caster sugar
1 teacup of mixed dried fruit
Milk to mix

Grease two 18cm (7 inch) sandwich tins. Sift flour, bicarbonate, and cream of tartar into large mixing bowl. Rub butter into these ingredients. Mix in the rest of the ingredients, adding sufficient milk to make a consistency of a soft dough. Transfer mixture into the two sandwich tins, and bake in preheated oven 200C, 400F, Gas Mark 6 for 15–20 minutes. Or you can make one large scone, baking for 35–40 minutes. Cool in a folded napkin and serve warm with butter.

EASTER BISCUITS

75g (3oz) butter
75g (3oz) caster sugar
1 egg yolk
175g (6oz) plain flour
2 tbsp milk
½ level tsp baking powder
½ level tsp cinnamon and ginger
50g (2oz) currants
50g (2oz) sultanas
25g (1oz) finely chopped mixed peel

Beat together the butter and sugar until light and fluffy. Then beat in the egg yolk and then the milk. Fold in the sifted flour with the cinnamon, ginger, baking powder and a pinch of salt. Add the currants, sultanas and peel, mix thoroughly and then set aside in a plastic bag and refrigerate for 1 hour. Then knead gently on a floured surface, and roll out to a thickness of 3mm (1/8th inch). Cut into rounds with a 5cm (2 inch) cutter and place on a greased tray. Bake on centre shelf of a preheated oven 200C, 400F, Gas Mark 6 for 10 minutes. Then brush biscuits with egg white and sprinkle with caster sugar and bake for a further 8–10 minutes until they are a golden brown.

GINGERNUTS

110g (4oz) self-raising flour
1 tsp ground ginger
1 level tsp bicarbonate of soda
35g (1½oz) granulated sugar
50g (2oz) margarine
50g (2oz) golden syrup

Sieve together the flour, bicarbon-ate of soda and ginger. Add sugar and rub in the margarine until mixture is crumbly. Add syrup and mix to a stiff paste. Roll into 16–18 balls and place, well spaced, on a baking sheet, flatten with a fork and bake in preheated oven 190C, 375F, Gas Mark 5 for 15 to 20 minutes.

CHOCOLATE BISCUITS

Delicious with coffee!

25g (1oz) cocoa
110g (4oz) plain flour
50g (2oz) caster sugar
50g (2oz) margarine
1 tbsp golden syrup
1 tsp bicarbonate of soda
Vanilla essence

Melt the margarine and golden syrup in a pan. Mix in the flour, cocoa, sugar and bicarbonate of soda, and vanilla. Beat well until smooth. Roll out and cut into rounds with a 5cm (2 inch) cutter. Prick biscuits with a fork and bake in preheated oven 190C, 375F, Gas Mark 5 for 15 minutes until crisp and cooked.

MACAROONS

110g (4oz) caster sugar
50g (2oz) ground almonds
1 tsp ground rice
White of a large egg
Few drops of almond essence
Whole almonds

Mix sugar, ground almonds and ground rice, add the almond essence and the unbeaten white of an egg. Mix to a fairly stiff paste, adding a little water if necessary. Beat thoroughly. Place teaspoons of the mixture on rice paper spread on a baking tray, and lightly brush with water to give a glaze. Place one split, blanched almond on top of each biscuit and bake in preheated oven 180C, 350F, Gas Mark 4 for 25 minutes until lightly brown and crisp.

FLAPJACKS

110g (4oz) butter
175g (6oz) porridge oats
50g (2oz) caster sugar
50g (2oz) demerara sugar

Melt butter in saucepan over gentle heat. Stir in the oats and sugar and spoon mixture into Swiss roll tin and press down lightly (or you can use a 20cm (8 inch) sponge tin). Bake in preheated oven 160C, 325F, Gas Mark 3 for 45–50 minutes, until golden brown. Cut into bars or segments while still hot, and leave in tin until cold before turning out. Store in an airtight tin.

OATCAKES

These oatcakes are good with a wedge of cheese and a plate of pickles.

450g (1lb) medium oatmeal
25g (1oz) butter or margarine
½ tsp bicarbonate of soda
½ tsp salt
300ml (½ pint) hot water

Melt butter or margarine in hot water. Add baking soda and salt to the oatmeal and mix together in a large bowl. Make a well in the centre of oatmeal and pour in the melted fat and water and mix to a fairly moist dough. Roll out dough thinly on a well dusted working surface, dusting with oatmeal to prevent sticking, and cut into rounds with a 8cm (3 inch) pastry cutter. Place on lightly greased baking sheets, and bake in preheated oven 180C, 350F, Gas Mark 4 for about 20–25 minutes until the oatcakes are crisp and golden.

SUFFOLK RUSKS

225g (8oz) self-raising flour
Pinch of salt
75g (3oz) butter
1 egg
Milk or water to mix

Sift flour and salt together. Rub in the butter lightly and mix with beaten egg and just enough milk or water to make a smooth dough. Roll out lightly, to about 2.5cm (1 inch) thick and cut into 6cm (2½ inch) rounds. Place on a baking sheet and cook in preheated oven 230C, 450F, Gas Mark 8 for 10 minutes. Remove from oven and split in half by hand. Replace on baking sheet with cut side upwards and bake for a further 10 to 15 minutes at 190C, 375F, Gas Mark 5, until crisp and golden. Cool, and serve with butter and cheese, or jam. These rusks store very well in an airtight tin.

Tea Breads, Soda Breads & Yeast Breads Rolls & Fruit Loaves

DATE BREAD

110g (4oz) dates, chopped
200ml (7floz) boiling water
1 tsp bicarbonate of soda
50g (2oz) butter or margarine
150g (5oz) soft brown sugar
200g (7oz) plain flour
1 tsp baking powder
1 tsp vanilla essence
25g (1oz) chopped walnuts
1 egg

Place chopped dates in basin and sprinkle with bicarbonate of soda. Pour on the boiling water and leave whilst preparing the other ingredients. Cream butter and sugar. Add egg. Mix in dry ingredients alternately with dates and water. Add vanilla and beat well. Place in a well greased loaf tin and bake in preheated oven 180C, 350F, Gas Mark 4.

BANANA BREAD

225g (8oz) plain flour
3 level tsp baking powder
1 tea cup mashed bananas
1 egg
50g (2oz) caster sugar
Pinch of salt
Grated rind of 1 lemon
50g (2oz) margarine
Add enough milk to make a soft,
    but not runny mixture

Sieve the dry ingredients except sugar. Rub in the margarine, then add the egg, sugar, lemon rind and mashed bananas. Mix thoroughly, adding a little milk as required. Put into a greased and floured 450g (1lb) loaf tin and bake for approximately 45 minutes in the centre of a preheated oven 180C, 350F, Gas Mark 4 until golden brown. Turn onto wire tray after 5 minutes and allow to cool. This loaf should be eaten within about four to five days, as the bananas in the mixture can go stale, but we find no difficulty in consuming it in our house!

TREACLE BREAD

This bread is popular with children, hot from the oven and spread with butter!

450g (1lb) plain flour
2 tbsp treacle
200ml (7floz) milk
1½ tbsp sugar
A good pinch ground ginger
½ tsp salt
1 tsp cream of tartar
1 tsp bicarbonate of soda

Heat treacle until it liquefies and add to the milk. Mix all the dry ingredients together. Moisten with the liquid to make a soft dough. Shape into a round shape, 1½ inch thick, score into quarters with a floured knife and put onto a baking sheet and bake in preheated oven 200C, 400F, Gas Mark 6 for approximately 40 minutes.

SODA BREAD

450g (1lb) plain flour
25g (1oz) butter or margarine
1 heaped tsp salt
200ml (7floz) buttermilk
1 heaped tsp bicarbonate of soda

Rub the butter into the flour. Add the salt and soda, mix well together by running the dry ingredients through your fingers. Add the buttermilk, and stir into a soft dough. Then knead lightly into a ball and turn out on to a lightly-floured baking-sheet. Flatten the dough into a circle about 1½ inches thick, make a cross in the centre with a floured knife, and bake in preheated oven at 220C, 425F, Gas Mark 7 for 30–35 minutes.

SAVOURY SODA BREAD

450g (1lb) wholemeal flour
1 tsp bicarbonate of soda
2 tsps salt
1 tbsp mixed dried herbs
50g (2oz) Cheddar cheese, grated
2 small onions, grated
300ml (½ pint) milk

Mix together the flour, soda, salt, herbs and cheese in a large mixing bowl. Add the onions and make a well in the centre and pour in the milk. Mix to make a soft dough and knead until smooth. Divide the dough in half and shape into two round loaves. Place on greased baking trays and cut a large cross in the top of each loaf. Bake in preheated oven 190C, 375F, Gas Mark 5 for 45–50 minutes until risen and brown and crusty. Cool on a wire tray and serve warm.

BASIC WHITE BREAD

Makes 1 x 900g (2lb) or 2 x 450g (1lb) loaves

700g (1½lb) strong plain flour
1 tsp salt
15g (½oz) lard
1 sachet easy blend dried yeast
 (or 20g (¾oz) fresh yeast)
425ml (15floz) hand hot water
Beaten egg or milk to glaze

Sift the flour and salt into a bowl. Rub in lard. Stir in the dried yeast then add the water. (If using fresh yeast, dissolve in a little hand hot water, then add to the flour with the remaining liquid.) Mix ingredients together to form a dough. Turn the mixture onto a floured surface and knead together for 5 minutes or until smooth and elastic. Place the dough in a lightly oiled plastic bag and leave in a warm place until doubled in size. Turn the dough onto a floured surface and knead again. Leave whole if making 1 loaf or cut in half if making 2 smaller loaves. Shape and place in greased loaf tins. Cover and leave to prove in a warm place until well risen. Glaze bread with beaten egg or milk and bake in preheated oven 240C, 475F, Gas Mark 9, until loaf is risen, well-browned and shrinking slightly from sides of the tin. Loaf should sound hollow when tapped on the bottom.

WHOLEMEAL BREAD

Makes one 900g (2lb) loaf or two 450g (1lb) loaves.

25g (1oz) fresh yeast or 1 level
   tbsp dried yeast and 1 level tsp
   caster sugar
425ml (¾pt) warm water
700g (1½lb) wholemeal flour
1 level tbsp caster sugar
1 level tbsp salt
25g (1oz) margarine

Mix fresh yeast with 150ml (¼pt) warm water. (If using dried yeast dissolve 1 level tsp of sugar in 150ml (¼pt) warm water and sprinkle over the dried yeast.) Leave until frothy. Place the flour, salt and 1 level tbsp caster sugar in a large mixing bowl and rub in the margarine. Stir in the yeast liquid with enough remaining water to give a soft dough. Knead well on a lightly floured surface for about 5 to 10 minutes, until the dough is smooth. Place the dough in a lightly floured mixing bowl and cover with cling film. Leave in warm place to rise and until the dough has doubled in size. Re-knead the dough to knock it back to its original size, and beat with your fist to knock out any air bubbles. Divide the dough in half and shape to fit two 450g (1lb) loaf tins, or use the whole dough to fit a 900g (2lb) tin. Brush the top of the bread with a little oil. Cover the tin or tins with cling film and leave in a warm place until the dough has risen to the top of the tins. Brush the bread with a little milk and bake in the preheated oven 230C, 450F, Gas Mark 8 for 30 to 40 minutes for a 900g (2lb) loaf or 25 to 30 minutes for the 450g (1lb) loaves or until the bread sounds hollow when tapped underneath. Turn out and cool on a wire tray.

GRANARY BREAD

Makes 2 x 900g (2lb) loaves

900g (2lb) Granary flour
2 tsp salt
45g (1½oz) lard
2 satchets easy blend dried yeast
600ml (1 pint) hand hot water
Beaten egg or milk to glaze

Place the flour and salt in a bowl and rub in the fat. Stir in the dried yeast, then add the water. Mix together. Turn the mixture onto a floured surface and knead together for 5 minutes, until smooth and elastic. Place the dough in a lightly oiled plastic bag and leave in a warm place until doubled in size. Turn the dough out onto a floured surface and knead again. Cut in half, reshape and place in 2 x 900g (2lb) greased loaf tins. Leave to prove again in a warm place until well risen. Meanwhile, preheat oven 240C, 475F, Gas Mark 9 for 5–7 minutes. Glaze loaves with beaten egg or milk and cook until the bread is browned, and shrinking from the sides of the tin, about 30–40 minutes. When turned out and tapped on the base, the loaf should sound hollow.

BREAD ROLLS

900g (2lb) plain flour
1 packet dried yeast
600ml (1pt) water
25g (1oz) margarine

Put 4 tbsp of the warm water in a small bowl with a tbsp of sugar. Sprinkle on the dried yeast, stirring. Put aside to activate. Rub margarine into the flour. Add yeast and the rest of the water. Knead well. Put aside to rise in a warm place for about 1 hour. Shape into small round knobs. Put on a greased baking tin, leave for 10 minutes and bake in preheated oven at 200C, 400F, Gas Mark 6 for about 15 minutes. These go well served hot with salads and soups.

OLIVE OIL ROLLS WITH SUN-DRIED TOMATOES

Makes 12 rolls or one loaf.

55g (2oz) sun-dried tomatoes in
   oil, drained and chopped
200ml (⅓ pint) boiling water
450g (1lb) strong white flour
2.5ml (½ tsp salt)
15ml (1 tbsp) sugar
1 satchet easy-blend yeast
5ml (1 tsp) oregano or mixed herbs
75ml (5 tbsp) olive oil, plus extra
   for greasing
1 egg, beaten

Put the tomatoes into a bowl with the boiling water and leave to soak for 10 minutes. Sift the flour and salt into a bowl, add the sugar, yeast and oregano or mixed herbs. Mix well and make a well in the centre. Add the oil to the well, together with the tomatoes and water. Reserve 1 tbsp beaten egg for glazing and add the remainder to the flour mixture. Mix well to form a dough. Knead the dough until smooth and elastic. Divide into 12 portions and shape into rolls. Place on greased baking sheets, cover with lightly oiled polythene and leave in a warm place to rise until doubled in size (about 1 hour). Meanwhile preheat the oven 240C, 475F, Gas Mark 9 for 5–7 minutes. Brush rolls lightly with the reserved egg and bake for 12–15 minutes. Serve warm or cold.

MALTED FRUIT LOAF

Stored in an airtight tin this loaf will keep for several days.

225g (8oz) self-raising flour
110g (4oz) mixed dried fruit
50g (2oz) caster sugar
50g (2oz) malted milk crystals
   (Bournvita type)
2 tbsp warmed golden syrup
150ml (¼pt) milk and water

Sieve flour into a large basin, then add the sugar, crystals and dried fruit. Mix all together and add the warmed syrup and enough milk and water to form a soft dropping consistency. Pour into a 450g (1lb) greased and lined loaf tin and bake in preheated oven 180C, 350F, Gas Mark 4 for about 1 hour, when the top of the loaf should be firm to the touch. To serve, cut into slices and spread with butter.

QUICK FRUIT AND NUT LOAVES

One of my quickest bread recipes – the mixture makes 2 x 450g (1lb) loaves.

450g (1lb) Granary Bread Meal
4 level tsp baking powder
350g (12oz) mixed dried fruit
25g (1oz) chopped walnuts
2 eggs, beaten
2 level tbsp marmalade
300ml (½pt) plus 4 tbsp strained
   tea

For the topping:
2 level dsp soft brown sugar
1 level dsp honey
25g (1oz) butter
25g (1oz) walnuts, chopped
**Melt all these ingredients
together in a saucepan**

Put the Granary Bread Meal into a mixing bowl and mix in the baking powder. Add the dried fruit and chopped walnuts then the beaten eggs, marmalade and tea. Stir well. Divide the mixture between the tins. Bake the loaves in preheated oven 180C, 350F, Gas Mark 4 for about 40 minutes; spoon topping over the loaves and put them back into the oven for 10 more minutes. Cool the loaves before turning them out of the tins. Store in an airtight tin – they keep very well. You can use hot tea for the mixture, in which case bake the loaves for about 5 minutes less.

Preserves

When jam and marmalade making time comes around I always make enough for not only my store cupboard, but extra so that I am able to give a few jars away to village bazaars and friends. So in all these preserve recipes you will find the yield is mostly for 4.5kg (10lb), but if you want to make less then just halve the ingredients which will give you about 2.25kg (5lb).

Always choose firm ripe fruit, as over-ripe fruit will not set. Blackcurrants, gooseberries, apples, plums and redcurrants are fruits that set well for jam making. Strawberries, raspberries, cherries and apricots have less pectin, and I always find extra lemon juice helps to make the fruit set. Rubbing the inside of your preserving pan with either glycerine or a small piece of butter or margarine, will help prevent the jam sticking, and prevent scum. One last tip ... use a preserving pan (or a large saucepan for small quantities) which is large enough, remembering that it should not be more than half full, so that when the fruit and sugar are combined together they can boil rapidly without the risk of boiling over.

BLACKBERRY JAM

2.7kg (6lb) blackberries
4 tbsp lemon juice
2.7kg (6lb) sugar

Wash blackberries gently and place in pan with the lemon juice. Simmer until the fruit is cooked and softened. Add the sugar and stir over a low heat until dissolved. Bring to the boil and boil rapidly until setting point is reached. Skim and pour into hot jars. Cover. Yield 4.5kg (10lb).

BLACKBERRY AND APPLE JAM

350g (12oz) cooking (or very sour)
    apples peeled and cored
300ml (½ pint) water
900g (2lb) blackberries
1.35kg (3lb) sugar

Slice the apples and poach them in 150ml (¼ pint) water until soft. Add cleaned blackberries and simmer in remainder of water until tender. Combine the two fruits together and add the sugar, heating gently until dissolved, then boil rapidly until setting point is reached. Skim, pour into warm dry jars and cover. Yield 2.25kg (5lb).

BLACKCURRANT JAM

1.8kg (4lb) blackcurrants
1.7ltrs (3 pints) water
2.7kg (6lb) sugar

Remove fruit from stalks and clean, rinsing and draining. Put fruit into preserving pan with water, and simmer slowly until the skins are tender. Add sugar and stir over a low heat until dissolved. Boil rapidly until setting point is reached. Test a little on a saucer to see if it has set, and when set, skim, and pour into warm dry jars and cover. Yields about 4.5kg (10lb).

APRICOT JAM

1.35kg (3lb) fresh apricots, washed
300ml (½ pint) water
2.7kg (6lb) sugar

Wash, halve and stone the fruit. Put into preserving pan with the water. Simmer until tender and the contents of the pan are reduced. Add the sugar and stir over a very low heat until completely dissolved. Bring to the boil, boiling rapidly until setting point is reached. Skim, pot and cover. Yields about 2.25kg (5lb).

APRICOT JAM (Dried Fruit)

This is a good jam to make during the winter months, when most fresh fruits are scarce.

450g (1lb) dried apricots
1.7 litres (3 pints) water
Juice of 1 lemon
1.35kg (3lb) sugar

Wash the apricots and put in a basin with the water, and soak overnight. Transfer the fruit and water to a preserving pan and simmer for 30 minutes, stirring every so often. Add the sugar and lemon juice, stirring over a low heat until the sugar is dissolved. Boil rapidly until setting point is reached. Skim, pot and cover. Yield approximately 2.25kg–2.7kg (5lb–6lb).

RASPBERRY JAM

A quick way of making this jam, it doesn't set too firmly, but has a delicious sharp and tangy flavour.

2.25kg (5lb) raspberries
2.7kg (6lb) granulated sugar

Bring the raspberries gently to the boil, and then boil rapidly for about 6 minutes. Remove from the heat; add the warmed sugar, stirring well over a low heat until all the sugar has dissolved. Bring to the boil and boil rapidly for 2 minutes. Skim, and pour the jam into dry, warm jars and cover. Yields about 4.5kg (10lb).

STRAWBERRY JAM

1.6kg (3½lb) strawberries, hulled
1.35kg (3lb) sugar
The juice of one large lemon

Heat the strawberries and lemon juice gently in the pan, stirring to reduce the volume. Add the sugar and stir until dissolved. Boil until setting point is reached (at this point you can add extra lemon juice if the jam is taking a while to set). Skim any scum off and set the jam aside for a while to allow the fruit to sink (about 15 mins). Stir gently to distribute the strawberries. Pour into warm, dry jars and cover immediately with waxed discs. Yields 2.25kg (5lb).

GOOSEBERRY JAM

1kg (2¼lb) gooseberries, washed
  and topped and tailed
1.35kg (3lb) sugar
425ml–600ml (¾–1pt) water

Put fruit into a pan with the water and simmer until the fruit is soft (about ¾hr). Then add the warmed sugar and stir over a low heat until dissolved. Bring to the boil and boil rapidly until setting point is reached, remove from heat after about 12 minutes rapid boiling and test on a saucer to see if it has set. Skim and pour into warm dry jars and cover. Yields about 2.25kg (5lb).

BLACKBERRY AND APPLE JELLY

1.8kg (4lb) blackberries
1.8kg (4lb) cooking apples
1.2 litres (2 pints) water
Sugar

Wash the apples and cut into quarters without peeling or coring. Simmer the blackberries and apples separately in the water for about 1 hour until fruits are tender. Mash well and allow to drip through a jelly bag. Measure the juice into a pan and bring to the boil, then stir in the sugar allowing 450g (1lb) sugar to each pint of juice. Boil briskly until set. Pour into warm jars and cover.

NOTE: It is difficult to give an exact yield for jelly because the losses vary in straining the juice, but as a guide, 4.5kg (10lb) of jelly is usually made from 2.7kg (6lb) sugar.

RASPBERRY JELLY

2.7kg (6lb) raspberries
Sugar

Put the raspberries in the pan (no water is needed) and heat through gently until fruit is quite soft. Crush the fruit well and strain through a jelly bag. Return the measured juice to the clean pan and bring to the boil. Add 450g (1lb) sugar to each 600ml (pint) of juice. Stir until sugar is dissolved and boil rapidly until setting point is reached. Pour into warmed jars and cover.

REDCURRANT JELLY

2.7kg (6lb) redcurrants
Sugar

Pick over fruit removing stems and leaves, and place in a preserving pan without any water. Heat through gently until currants are soft and cooked (about 1hr). Mash, then strain the pulp through a jelly bag, leaving it to drip. Measure the juice into a clean pan and add 560g (1¼lb) of sugar to each 600ml (pint) of juice. Bring to the boil, continually stirring, and then boil for 1 minute without stirring. Skim the jelly and pour quickly into warm jars, making sure it does not set at the bottom of the pan, and cover.

MINT JELLY

1.35kg (3lb) green cooking apples
Water and vinegar
Fairly large bunch of fresh mint
Sugar
3 level dsp chopped mint
A few drops of green colouring
  (optional)

Wash apples, but do not peel or core, cut into quarters and put into preserving pan. Cover with water and vinegar in equal parts with the bunch of mint. Simmer until apples are completely soft, then boil for 5 minutes. Strain overnight through a jelly bag, and the next day put all the juice into a preserving pan and add 450g (1lb) sugar for each 600ml (pint) of juice, and boil rapidly, stirring until sugar is dissolved, then add the chopped mint and green colouring, and boil until setting point is reached. Pour into hot jars and cover with waxed discs.

SEVILLE MARMALADE

A recipe that produces a nice chunky marmalade, and is quick and simple to make.

1.35kg (3lb) Seville oranges
1.25lts (4 pints) water
Juice of 2 lemons
2.7kg (6lb) sugar

Wash the fruit and put it whole and unpeeled into a preserving pan. Pour on the water and bring to the boil, then simmer with the lid on the pan until the fruit is tender, about 1½–2hrs. When fruit has cooled cut it in half and remove pips, and cut the fruit up, retaining all the juice. Return the pips to the water and boil for a further 6 minutes. Put the sliced oranges with the liquid (strained free from pips) and adding the lemon juice into the preserving pan. Reduce the heat and add warmed sugar and stir until dissolved. Bring to a quick boil and boil rapidly until setting point is reached. Yield 4.5kg (10lb).

GRAPEFRUIT MARMALADE

1.35kg (3lb) grapefruit
4 lemons
6 pints water
2.7kg (6lb) sugar

Wash the fruit and cut into half, and squeeze out the juice. Remove some of the pith if necessary, and cut it up and put with the pips in a muslin bag. Finely slice the peel, then transfer all the fruit and juice into a bowl with the water, cover and leave overnight. The next day put it all into a preserving pan and gently simmer for 1½–2hrs until the peel is soft. Remove muslin bag, add the sugar and stir until it is all dissolved, and boil rapidly until setting point is reached. Pour into prepared warm pots and cover. Yield 4.5kg (10lb).

LEMON CURD

I always make lemon curd in small quantities, as it is not a good 'keeper', but if you want to make a larger batch just double the quantity of ingredients, and again yields can vary, but this recipe usually makes 700g–900g (1½–2lb).

3 lemons
4 eggs
75g (3oz) butter
225g (8oz) caster sugar

Melt the butter in a basin over a saucepan of boiling water. Add the sugar and the grated rind and juice of the 3 lemons. Beat the eggs and add to the mixture, stir continuously with a wooden spoon until thick (be careful not to boil).

MINCEMEAT

Makes 1.8kg (4lb)

225g (8oz) raisins
225g (8oz) currants
175g (6oz) sultanas
50g (2oz) blanched almonds
110g (4oz) chopped mixed candied
  peel
110g (4oz) shredded peel
225g (8oz) soft brown sugar
2 large cooking apples
Grated rind and juice of 1 large
  lemon
½ level tsp mixed spice
½ level tsp cinnamon
4 tbsp brandy or rum

Peel, core and coarsely grate apples. Chop almonds. Mix all ingredients together thoroughly. Leave covered for one day, turning mixture over with a wooden spoon throughout the day. Turn into clean dry jam jars, cover with waxed circles and transparent covers. Store in a cool, dry, dark cupboard.

Chutneys and Pickles

Making chutney consists mainly of just chopping and cooking, with lovely aromas wafting thro' the kitchen, and having the satisfaction of seeing neatly stacked jars of the fruits of summer and autumn stored in rows in my cupboard, in fact chutney making couldn't be easier.

PEAR CHUTNEY

1.35kg (3lb) cooking pears, unpeeled
450g (1lb) cooking apples, unpeeled
700g (1½lb) onions, peeled
225g (8oz) seedless raisins
110g (4oz) sultanas
110g (4oz) currants
450g (1lb) brown sugar
1 tbsp black treacle

600ml (1pt) malt vinegar
1 tbsp salt
Pinch of cayenne pepper

Wipe over pears and apples, and chop together with onions. Put all the ingredients in a saucepan and cook until thick – about 1 hour. Pot into warm jars and cover.

GOOSEBERRY CHUTNEY

900g (2lb) green gooseberries
450g (1lb) brown sugar
450g (1lb) white sugar
1 large onion
450g (1lb) dates
450g (1lb) sultanas
50g (2oz) salt
2 large cups of malt vinegar

Simmer gooseberries in vinegar until soft. Chop dates and onions finely (I usually chop mine in a food processor with the other ingredients.) Boil until a thick consistency and pot up in warmed jars and cover. Yields about 2.7kg (6lb).

MARROW CHUTNEY

900g (2lb) marrow
450g (1lb) sugar
225g (8oz) onions
225g (8oz) apples
225g (8oz) seedless raisins
600ml (1 pint) vinegar
A few cloves
25g (1oz) mustard seeds
35g (1½oz) crushed whole ginger
25g (1oz) chillies
50g (2oz) salt

Peel the marrow, take out the

seeds, cut marrow into small cubes. Place in bowl with the salt and allow to stand for 24 hours. Strain liquid from marrow. Put marrow into preserving pan with peeled and chopped onions, apple, sugar, raisins, vinegar and spices tied in a muslin bag. Bring to the boil and simmer until cooked to consistency required (1–2hrs) stirring frequently. Allow to cool a little and then pour into warm screw top jars.

GREEN TOMATO CHUTNEY

1.35kg green tomatoes
4 large cooking apples
2 small cucumbers
3 large onions
175g (6oz) sultanas
350g (¾lb) demerara sugar
2 tbsp mustard
1½ tsp ground ginger
1 level tsp cayenne pepper
1½ tbsp salt

700ml (1¼ pints) malt vinegar

Remove stalks from tomatoes. Peel and slice onions and apples, slice cucumbers and put all the ingredients into a large preserving pan. Bring to the boil and allow to simmer for 2½–3 hours, until quite soft, stirring frequently. Pour into prepared warmed jars and cover.

RIPE TOMATO CHUTNEY

This chutney is more like a sauce, and goes well with fish, hot or cold, as well as most meat dishes.

3.6kg (8lb) ripe tomatoes
450g (1lb) onions, peeled and
   sliced
75g (3oz) salt
10g (½oz) cloves
Cayenne pepper and ground
   ginger to taste, I usually use
   ¾ tsp of each
600ml (1 pint) vinegar
175g (6oz) sugar

Cut tomatoes into halves, put into a large pan with all the other ingredients and bring to the boil. Simmer for about 2½ hours, and then put through a sieve until only the seeds and skin remains. Return liquid to pan and add the vinegar and sugar and boil for a further ½ hour until the chutney is thickened.

APPLE CHUTNEY

1.8 kilos (4lb) apples (windfalls are
   ideal)
900g (2lb) onions, sliced
225g (8oz) sugar
225g (8oz) sultanas
Salt
Cayenne pepper
600ml (1 pint) spiced vinegar

Core and chop the apples, add the sliced onions, sugar and sultanas. Sprinkle with a tbsp salt and a pinch of cayenne pepper. Cover with 600ml (1 pint) spiced vinegar and simmer gently for 2 hours, stirring frequently. Pour into warmed jars and cover.

SAGE JELLY

Delicious with roast duck or pork.

900g (2lb) cooking apples, peeled
   and cored
150ml (¼ pint) water
12 fresh leaves of sage
Sugar
Colouring

Slice apples and simmer in water until reduced to a pulp. Strain through a jelly bag and measure – to each 600ml (pint) of juice allow 350g (¾lb) sugar. Put juice and sugar into a preserving pan with the sage tied in a bunch, and bring slowly to the boil until it sets when tested. Remove bunch of sage, add enough green colouring to tint. Pot into small warmed jars and cover.

RUNNER BEAN CHUTNEY

900g (2lb) kidney beans, peeled
   and sliced
4–5 medium onions, peeled and
   chopped
700g (1½lb) demerara sugar
1½ tbsp turmeric
1½ tbsp mustard
1½ tbsp cornflour
900ml (1½ pints) malt vinegar

Put beans and onions into a large pan in enough salt water to cover them and bring to the boil, then simmer until tender. Strain and drain well and cut up as small as possible, or you can put through a food processor for a few minutes, taking care not to liquidise it. Add the sugar and 700ml (1¼ pints) of vinegar and boil for 15 minutes. Mix the turmeric, mustard and corn flour with the other 150ml (¼ pint) of vinegar and add to the beans and onions and boil for another 15 minutes. Allow to cool and pour into warmed jars and cover.

PICCALILLI

2 cauliflowers (not too large)
2 medium-sized cucumbers
16 young French beans
450g (1lb) onions
1 medium sized marrow
1.2ltrs (2 pints) vinegar
25g (1oz) whole spice
110g (¼lb) demerara sugar
10g (½oz) ground ginger
25g (1oz) mustard
10g (½oz) turmeric
1 tbsp plain flour

Cut all the vegetables into small pieces lie on a large dish and sprinkle with salt. Leave for 12 hours. Drain off water, and then boil vinegar (leaving a small quantity of vinegar) with the spice, then strain. Mix the other ingredients with the remaining cold vinegar into a smooth paste, and then mix with the boiled vinegar. Pour into a large saucepan, add vegetables and boil for 15–20 minutes. Allow to cool and pour into warmed jars and cover.

PICKLED PEARS

4.5kg (10lb) pears
1.35kg (3lb) demerara sugar
600ml (1 pint) vinegar
25g (1oz) cloves

Put sugar, vinegar and cloves into a large pan and boil for about 15 minutes, then strain. Peel pears and cut into small portions, transfer to pan and boil in vinegar mixture until tender. Put into warm screw-top jars.

PICKLED ONIONS

A quantity of small onions
Sufficient malt vinegar to cover
To each 1.2ltrs (2 pints) of vinegar
    allow 2 tsp allspice and 2 tsp
    whole black peppercorns

Peel onions and put into clean dry jars. Boil the vinegar with spices and when **cold** pour it over the onions to fill the jars completely. Cover and store in a cool dry place. The onions should be ready in two weeks, but if you have used hot vinegar then they will be ready earlier.

PICKLED GREEN CABBAGE

Cut up finely 1 large cabbage and 4 large onions, sprinkle with salt and allow to stand for at least 24 hours. Drain well through a colander or sieve, and then boil slowly in 1–1½ litres (2 pints) of vinegar for 25 minutes. Mix together 1 cupful of plain flour, 2 cupfuls of sugar, 2 tsps of curry powder and 2 tbsp of mustard in 600ml (1 pint) of vinegar. Pour over the cabbage and boil all together for another 5 minutes. Bottle while hot, and leave until cold, then cover in the usual way.

PICKLED EGGS

These are delicious when eaten with cold meat or cheese, and are ideal to take on a picnic.

16 hardboiled eggs
1.2ltrs (2 pints) vinegar
10g (½oz) black peppercorns
10g (½oz) allspice
10g (½oz) whole ginger

Remove egg shells and place eggs in wide-necked jars. Bring to the boil the peppercorns, spice and ginger in the vinegar for 10 minutes, pour it, while boiling hot, over the eggs. When cold cover closely and store in a cool dry place. These are ready for use in about fortnight.

Drinks and Sweetmeats

DRINKS

LEMONADE

25g (1oz) citric acid
900g (2lb) granulated sugar
1.5 litres (2½ pints) boiling water
2 lemons

Grate zest of lemon, cut and extract juice. Place in a large bowl the rind and lemons with the citric acid and granulated sugar and pour over this the boiling water, stirring until the sugar dissolves. When cool add the lemon juice. Leave overnight. The next day strain very carefully into washed screw-top bottles. This lemonade keeps well in a cool place for several weeks, and is a very refreshing drink on a hot summer's day

SOMERSET CIDER FRUIT CUP

Makes 16 glasses

1 large bottle of Somerset cider
2 small bottles ginger ale
2 small bottles tonic water
1 medium tin grapefuit juice
300ml (½ pint) fresh orange juice
1 small bottle maraschino cherries

Mix all ingredients together in a large bowl with strained cherries. Pour into glass jugs and garnish with strips of cucumber skin and slices of orange and lemon.

CHAMPAGNE COCKTAIL

1 bottle of Champagne
1 liqueur glass Cointreau
1 liqueur or sherry glass of dry
   Martini
2 sherry glasses wine brandy

Dash of bitters

Mix all the ingredients together, taste while mixing, and keep off the road for 24 hours!

ELDERFLOWER CORDIAL

This is a delicious and refreshing drink, and easy to prepare.

40 heads of elderflowers
1.8kg (4lb) sugar (or less
   according to taste)
75g (3oz) citric acid
2 lemons squeezed and chopped
1.7 litres (3 pints) boiling water

Mix all the ingredients together in a large bowl. Stir each day for 5 days. Strain and bottle. Keep in refrigerator. To keep for a long period put into suitable containers and freeze.

BLACKBERRY WINE

This is a very inexpensive drink, and the wine will keep in a good condition for 12 months, having a flavour rather like that of a good port wine.

Place alternate layers of ripe blackberries and sugar in a wide-necked jar and allow to stand for 3 weeks. Then strain off the liquid and bottle, adding a couple of raisins to each bottle. Cork lightly at first and later more tightly.

ORANGE GIN

This drink has quite a kick in it, and is ideal on a cold winter's day after a brisk walk!

1 bottle of gin
225g (8oz) unrefined sugar
1¼ Seville oranges
1¼ lemons

Cut peel of oranges and lemons very thinly into strips, removing all the pith. Put gin, peel and sugar into a covered jar and stir well for 10 minutes every day for two weeks, using a wooden spoon. Strain, bottle and keep for a year (if you can) before using. If you want to make a larger quantity just double the ingredients.

SWEETMEATS

Try making your own sweets, it's not too difficult, and the majority of sweets are made by boiling a sugar syrup, and for this a sugar-boiling thermometer is needed.

General guidelines:

1. Use a strong, heavy saucepan, large enough to prevent the syrup boiling over.
2. Be accurate over all weighing and measuring.
3. See that the sugar is completely dissolved before the syrup is allowed to boil.
4. After boiling point has been reached, do not stir the syrup (unless directed to in the recipe).

Various stages between boiling point and caramel can be recognised by the following simple tests – standard syrup 450g (1lb) sugar to 150ml (¼ pint) water:

Used for making soft centres:

Soft ball (235F–245F) when a drop of the syrup is put into very cold water, it forms a soft ball; at 235F the soft ball flattens on removal from water, but the higher the temperature, the firmer the ball, till it reaches the firm ball stage.

Used for making fondants and fudge:

Hard ball (245F–265F): the syrup when dropped into cold water, forms a ball which is hard enough to hold its shape, but is still pliable.

Used for making caramels and marshmallows:

Soft crack (270F–290F): the syrup, when dropped into cold water, separates into threads which are hard, but not brittle.

Used for toffees:

Hard crack (300F–310F): when a drop of the syrup is put into cold water, it separates into threads which are hard and brittle.

Used for hard toffees and rocks:

Caramel (310F): the syrup turns golden-brown.

Centigrade Table (approximate)

235–245F 130C	270–290F 150C
245–265F 130C	300–310F 150C

COCONUT ICE

Dissolve 450g (1lb) granulated sugar in 150ml (¼ pint) water and boil to a syrup, heating it until it reaches a temperature of 240F. Remove the pan from the heat and add 110g (4oz) grated or desiccated coconut. Stir until the mixture thickens, then quickly pour half into a greased tin; colour the remainder pink, pour it on to the white "ice", and leave to set. When it is cool, cut into bars.

PEPPERMINT CREAMS

450g (1lb) icing sugar
¼ tsp cream of tartar
2 tsp lemon juice
1 egg white
Peppermint essence

Sift icing sugar and cream of tartar into a bowl. Add the lemon juice and just enough egg white to make a firm paste. Flavour well with peppermint essence, put into a plastic bag and leave for one hour. Roll out on a board which has been liberally dusted with sieved icing sugar. Cut into 2.5cm (1") circles, 5mm (¼ inch) thick. Cover creams with a sheet of greaseproof paper and leave overnight to dry. This recipe makes 450g (1lb), and makes an attractive gift packed in a cellophane bag, and tied with a red satin ribbon.

MARSHMALLOWS

275g (10oz) granulated sugar
1 dsp glucose
300ml (½ pint) water
20g (¾oz) powdered gelatine
1 egg white
1–2 tbsps orange flower water or
    rose water
Icing sugar

Dissolve sugar and glucose in 150ml (¼ pint) water and boil to 130C, 260F. Meanwhile, dissolve the gelatine in another 150ml (¼ pint) water to keep warm. Whisk the egg white stiffly. Put the gelatine in a basin and pour on the boiling syrup, whisking all the time. Add the orange flower water and then the egg white, still whisking, and continue to whisk until the mixture is stiff and thick – it may take 20–25 minutes. While it is still liquid, pour it into a tin which has been lined with greaseproof paper and dredged with icing sugar. When the marshmallow is set, cut it up with scissors, roll it in icing sugar and leave to dry for at least 24 hours.

SIMPLE FRENCH NOUGAT

Rice paper
110g (4oz) blanched almonds
50g (2oz) angelica
450g (1lb) sugar
225g (8oz) glucose
150ml (¼ pint) water
2 egg whites

Line a tin with rice paper. Brown the almonds in the oven, then chop them roughly, with the angelica. Meanwhile boil the sugar, glucose and water to 140C, 270F. Beat the egg whites until they are stiff, then gradually beat in the syrup. As soon as the mixture begins to thicken, add the chopped angelica and browned nuts. Mix well, then pour the mixture into the prepared tin. Cover with another piece of rice paper and press down with a heavy weight. Leave the nougat for at least 12 hours before cutting it into bars; wrap the pieces of nougat in waxed or transparent paper.

VANILLA FUDGE

450g (1lb) granulated sugar
50g (2oz) butter or margarine
150ml (¼ pint) evaporated milk
150ml (¼ pint) water
A few drops of vanilla essence

Put all the ingredients, except the vanilla essence, into a large pan, and heat gently until the sugar has dissolved and the butter melted, then bring to the boil. Boil steadily, stirring, until a temperature of 130C, 240F is reached (or "soft ball" stage). Remove pan from the heat and add the essence, then beat well. Continue beating the mixture until it becomes thick and creamy, as the sugar "grains", then pour into a greased tin (about 15cm x 20.5cm) (6" x 8"). Leave the fudge to cool, and when nearly set, mark into squares with a sharp knife.

CHOCOLATE FUDGE

450g (1lb) granulated sugar
300ml (½ pint) fresh milk
25g (1oz) cocoa
1 tsp glucose
2 tbsp cream (optional)
50g (2oz) butter or margarine
½ vanilla essence

Dissolve the sugar in the milk, add all the remaining ingredients except the essence, and bring to the boil, stirring all the time. Heat to a temperature of 130C, 240F, add the essence and remove pan from the heat. Beat the mixture until it is thick and creamy, then finish as for the vanilla fudge above.

RUM TRUFFLES

225g (8oz) slab of plain chocolate
1 tbsp condensed milk
A few drops of rum
Chocolate vermicelli

Melt the chocolate, stirring all the time, then add the milk and rum. Beat well, and put in a cool place until it is stiff enough to handle. Form the mixture into small balls and roll them in chocolate vermicelli. Put the truffles into paper cases.

NUT TOFFEE

450g (1lb) brown sugar
150ml (¼ pint) water
25g (1oz) butter
2 tbsp golden syrup
¼ tsp cream of tartar
2–3 drops acetic acid or 1 tsp
   vinegar
75g (3oz) chopped almonds or
   walnuts

Put the sugar and water into a pan and heat gently to dissolve the sugar. Bring to the boil and add butter, syrup, cream of tartar and acetic acid. Cover, and boil again for a few minutes. Remove lid and heat to 150C, 300F. Pour into a greased tin, sprinkle with the nuts, and leave to set. When half-set, mark into squares, break it into pieces when it is quite cold.

IMPERIAL/METRIC EQUIVALENTS

Many people get confused with metric measurements. This isn't surprising when you think that one ounce is equivalent to 28.5 grammes and one fluid ounce converts to 28.5 millilitres. To try and make things slightly easier I have rounded all the metric measurements up or down to the nearest 5 grammes or 5 millilitres, but in some cases I have used The Guild of Food Writers' metrication chart, which I use for reference. Basically the Guild takes a gram-friendly policy – taking convenient metric weights and giving the UK equivalent in a less user-friendly amount. Either way you can't go wrong as I have given the UK Imperial measurements in all the recipes.

WEIGHT

The Imperial pound (lb) approximately equals 450 g—slightly less than ½ kilogram (500 g).

Imperial	Approx. metric equivalent
1 oz	25 g
2 oz	50 g
3 oz	75 g
4 oz	100–125 g
5 oz	150 g
6 oz	175 g
7 oz	200 g
8 oz	225 g
9 oz	250 g
10 oz	275 g
11 oz	300 g
12 oz	325–350 g
13 oz	375 g
14 oz	400 g
15 oz	425 g
16 oz (1 lb)	450 g
1½ lb	700 g

LIQUID CAPACITY

The Imperial pint (20 fluid oz) measures slightly more than ½ litre—approximately 575 millilitres (ml).

Imperial	Approx. metric equivalent
1 fluid oz	25 ml
2 fluid oz	50 ml
3 fluid oz	75 ml
4 fluid oz	100–125ml
5 fluid oz	150 ml
6 fluid oz	175 ml
7 fluid oz	200 ml
8 fluid oz	225 ml
9 fluid oz	250 ml
10 fluid oz (½ pint)	275–300 ml
20 fluid oz (1 pint)	575–600 ml

OVEN TEMPERATURES

The thermostatic dials on some electric cookers are marked in Centigrade. These correspond to Fahrenheit and gas markings as follows:

°F	°C	Gas mark	Temperature
250	130	½	Very cool
275	140	1	Very cool
300	150	2	Cool
325	{ 160 / 170	3	Warm
350	180	4	Moderate
375	190	5	Fairly hot
400	200	6	Fairly hot
425	{ 210 / 220	7	Hot
450	230	8	Very hot
475	240	9	Very hot

AMERICAN MEASURES

1 pint	= 16 fluid oz	= 453 cc
1 cup	= 8 fluid oz	= 227 cc
½ cup	= 4 tablespoonfuls of fluid	
1 cup butter	= 5 oz	= 142 gms
1 cup grated cheese	= 3½ oz	= 98 gms
1 cup sugar	= 7½ oz	= 223 gms
1 cup flour	= 4½ oz	= 128 gms

GELATINE

1 oz gelatine will stiffen 1 pint fluid or fruit juice; ½ oz gelatine will stiffen 1 pint mayonnaise or thick sauce

Not all of "My Kind of People" featured in this book work in a hotel, tea room, or run their own business, but here is a list of names, addresses, tel. nos. etc., of the 14 who do!

Sally & Robert Bendall, Hollow Trees Farm Shop, Semer, Ipswich IP7 6HX. *Tel:* 01449 741247; *Fax:* 01449 741799; *E-mail:* sally@ hollowtrees.co.uk - *Website:* www. hollowtrees.co.uk - Opening times: Monday–Saturday 8.30am–5.45pm; Sundays and Bank Holidays 9am–5pm.

Sarah Boosé, Spencer's Farm Shop, Wickham St. Pauls, Halstead, Essex. *Tel:* 01787 269413. Open daily for fresh fruit, vegetables, eggs and other produce – open winter months with a selection of home grown apples. Opening times: Summer 9am–6pm. Winter 9am–5pm.

Regis Crepy, The Great House, Market Place, Lavenham, Suffolk CO10 9QZ. *Tel:* 01787 247431; *E-mail:* infor@greathouse.co.uk - *Website:* www.greathouse.co.uk

Sue & Richard Evans, Stonehouse Farm, West Harling, Norwich NR16 2SD. *Tel:* 01953 717258; *Fax:* 01953 717333; *E-mail:* stonehouse.farm@ farming.co.uk

Anne Faiers, Sparling & Faiers, Baking, Confectionery and Catering, 11 Market Place, Lavenham, Suffolk. *Tel:* 01787 247297.

Win Gage, Corn Craft, Monks Eleigh, Suffolk IP7 7AY. *Tel:* 01449 740456. Opening times: Monday to Saturday 10am to 5pm, Sunday 11am to 5pm. Open every day except Christmas Day, Boxing Day and New Year's Day.

Pam & Barry Gray, Willow Cottage Tea Rooms, Stocks Green, Castle Acre, Kings Lynn, Norfolk PE32 2AE. *Tel:* 01760 755551; *Fax:* 01760 755012; *E-mail:* gv33@dial.pipex. com - Tea Rooms are open from 10.30am. to 5.30pm Tuesday to Sunday and Bank Holiday Mondays. Bed & Breakfast – Twin-bedded & Double-bedded rooms.

John Heeks, A. R. Heeks & Sons, Grocers & Delicatessen, Licensed, 13 Market Place, Lavenham, Suffolk. *Tel:* 01787 247257. Open 8am–8pm Monday to Saturday. Closed Bank Holidays.

Eva King, The Angel, Country Inn and Restaurant Hotel, Market Place, Lavenham, Suffolk. *Tel:* 01787 247388; *Fax:* 01787 248344; *E-mail:* angellav@aol.com - *Website:* www.lavenham.co.uk/angel - Props: Roy and Anne Whitworth, John and Val Barry.

Meinir & Dewi, direct Welsh Lamb Ltd, Esgair Farm, Aberdyfi, Gwynedd LL35 0SP. Order hotline: 01654 767101. *Fax orders:* 01654 767102. *E-mail:* enquiries@ welshlambdirect.co.uk - *Website:* www.welshlambdirect.co.uk

Beth Raine, The Swan Hotel (Forte UK) Ltd, High Street, Lavenham, Suffolk CO10 9QA. *Tel:* 01787 247477; *Fax:* 01787 248286. *E-mail:* Heritagehotels-Lavenham.Swan@ fortehotels.com - *Website:* www. heritage-hotels.com

Theresa Tollemache & Abi Kelly, Volga Linen Company, Unit 1D, Eastland Road Industrial Estate, Leiston, Suffolk IP16 4LL. *Tel:* 01728 635020; *Fax:* 01728 635021; *Website:* www.i-i.net/volgalinen - *E-mail:* volgalinen@aol.com

Sue & Ian Whitehead, Lane Farm Country Foods, Lane Farm, Brundish, Suffolk IP13 8BW. *Tel & Fax:* 01379 384593; *E-mail:* ian@ lanefarm.co.uk - *Website:* www. lanefarm.co.uk

Felicity Pocock & John Youdell, Lakeland Hampers & Cumbrian Food Shop & Tea Room, 14 New Shambles, Kendal, Cumbria LA9 4TS. *Tel & Fax:* 01539 730036; *E-mail:* sales@lakelandhampers. co.uk - *Website:* www.lakeland hampers.co.uk

FOR YOUR NOTES

FOR YOUR NOTES